The
DOCTRINES
Baptists Believe

[signature] '98, - FLOWER MOUND -

The
DOCTRINES
Baptists Believe

Roy T. Edgemon

Convention Press
Nashville, Tennessee

© Copyright 1988 • Convention Press
All rights reserved
6th reprint 1998

This book is the text for course CG-0148
in the subject area Baptist Doctrine
in the Christian Growth Study Plan

Dewey Decimal Classification Number: 230.6
Subject Heading: BAPTISTS — DOCTRINES

Printed in the United States of America

Adult Discipleship and Family Department
The Sunday School Board of the Southern Baptist Convention
127 Ninth Avenue, North
Nashville, Tennessee 37234

Contents

About the Author

A NATIVE OF TEXAS, DR. ROY T. EDGEMON IS THE director of the Discipleship and Family Development Division of the Sunday School Board of the Southern Baptist Convention. He was a pastor in Texas for 15 years before serving as a foreign missionary in Japan and then as director of evangelism planning and consultation for the Home Mission Board. He is a graduate of Midwestern University and Southwestern Baptist Theological Seminary. Since returning from Japan, Dr. Edgemon has served many churches as interim pastor while serving with the Home Mission Board and the Sunday School Board.

His wife, Anna Marie Edgemon, is a writer, teacher, and speaker who has been the Bible teacher for many state WMU conventions and has led conferences throughout the world. She recently spent the summer as a volunteer teaching at a university in China. The Edgemons have one daughter, Lori Shepard, a physical therapist. She is married to Douglas Shepard, who is with National Instruments of Austin, Texas. Both Lori and Douglas are the products of missionary homes. The Edgemons have one grandson, Nathan Roy Shepard, and one granddaughter, Sarah Elizabeth Shepard, to whom this book is dedicated.

Preface

MY CALLING AND MINISTRY ARE THOSE OF A preacher. I have a pastor's heart. For more than thirty-five years I have stood behind the sacred desk each Sunday and proclaimed the Word of God to people from all walks of life. I have tried to communicate to people in their present circumstances and to meet their specific needs. I have written this book with the same commitment. I have approached this task not as a theologian writing a textbook but as a pastor addressing his people.

This book, of course, does not deal with *all* the doctrines Baptists believe. Space limitations did not permit me to write all I would like to on the various topics. The book does represent one pastor's perspective on the key doctrines of our faith. For a more comprehensive study I commend to you the *Disciple's Study Bible*, which systematically traces twenty-seven doctrines through the Bible. My prayer is that you be rooted and grounded in sound doctrine and not be "tossed back and forth by the waves, and blown here and there by every wind of teaching" that comes along.

Roy T. Edgemon

CHAPTER 1

The Bible:
the Inspired Word of God

The word of God is living and active. Sharper than
any double-edged sword, it penetrates even to
dividing soul and spirit, joints and marrow; it judges
the thoughts and attitudes of the heart.
Hebrews 4:12

SOME YEARS AGO A PLAY WAS WRITten in Russia with the intent to mock Christianity. Its title was *Christ in Tuxedo*. The opening scene showed a bar in a church building with nuns in their habits standing at the bar drinking and gambling. The church was depicted as a den of iniquity. The actor who was to play the lead, a Russian star performer, was to walk on stage and to begin reading a few verses from Matthew 5, the Sermon on the Mount. He stood and began to read. Strangely, he could not stop. He continued to read on and on as though under an irresistible compulsion. A quietness fell over the actors, and a stillness fell over the crowd. Finally, the actor raised his hands and said: "Jesus, remember me when You come into Your Kingdom." The curtain fell permanently. The authorities never allowed it to be played again.[1] Even in mockery, the Word of God broke through the minds of the people. God's Word is alive.

Bible is a good word, and all of us understand that it refers to God's inspired, written Word. *Bible* comes from the Greek word *biblos*, meaning *book*. The Bible is *the* Book. My favorite term, though, is *Word of God*, the term used in Hebrews 4:12. *Word of God* has behind it a certain sense of authority and finality. The statement "thus saith the Lord" appears almost four hundred times in the Bible. What God speaks is His word, and the Bible is the written record of what God has spoken and done throughout history.

The writer of Hebrews was not the only one to use *Word of God*. Paul wrote, "Take the helmet of salvation and the sword of the Spirit, which is the word of God" (Eph. 6:17); and Peter wrote, "You have been born again . . . through the living and enduring word of God" (1 Pet. 1:23).

The Bible has much to say about itself. Hebrews 4:12 states four truths about the Word of God. Our concentration on the passage will help us organize that information.

God's Word: Divine in Origin

The first truth stated in this verse is that the Bible is divine in its origin. That is what *Word of God* means. Many centuries were required to put the Bible together, and numerous authors wrote it in sixty-six books under God's inspiration on papyrus and parchment and perhaps clay tablets, but this does not diminish the fact that it is God's Word. In fact, such intense human involvement throughout a long period of history tells us that God is a God of revelation.

John started his Gospel with a discussion of *logos*, which we translate as *Word*, to refer to Jesus. *Logos* has a long history among both Jews and Greeks. The Greeks used *logos* to refer to the principle of reason, and the word was heavy with the weight of Greek philosophy. Some scholars have believed that John had this use in mind when he called Jesus the *logos*. The view makes sense; Jesus is ultimate Reason. But that approach misses the rich Jewish heritage that was John's.

To the Jewish mind, *logos* referred to God's active power in history as history obeyed His command. God spoke, and history changed; God spoke, and blessing or judgment occurred; God spoke, and miracles happened. God spoke His law. God's speaking was so powerful that nothing could stop His word from taking its course. John called Jesus that Word. He was God's ultimate word of redemption, God's solution and comment on the human condition. Jesus is God's Word come to earth, God's moving in history, God's agent of judgment and blessing, God's power. Nothing can stop that Word; He has come, and history will move toward God's destiny for it. A word is the expression of a thought, and Jesus is the expression of the thoughts of God. He is very God.

On occasion, those who insist on the absolute authority and truthfulness of the written Word of God have been accused of bibliolatry, worshiping the Bible rather than the God who wrote it. We must admit that this error is possible, but we insist that the accusation is largely an empty one. Jesus is the Word of God; the Bible is the Word of God. They are not equal. Jesus is the One by whom we interpret the Bible. The Bible brings the reader into confrontation with Jesus Christ. To believe in the truth and authority of the Bible does not eclipse Jesus as the Word but rather reveals the Jesus of history and brings us under the convicting power of His living Word through the inspiration of the Holy Spirit. Our authoritative knowledge about Jesus is found in this Word; our authoritative knowledge about the nature of God is found in this Word. Without a doubt, God and Jesus are bigger than the Bible, but the Bible is the basis and benchmark of our knowledge and experience about all God is and says. The Bible as the Word of God has the power of Jesus' word behind it and in it.

The Bible makes its own assertions about its divine origin. Paul wrote, "All Scripture is God-breathed and is useful for teaching, rebuking, correcting and training in righteousness, so that the man of God may be thoroughly equipped for every good work" (2 Tim. 3:16-17). Peter wrote, "Prophecy never had its origin in the will of man, but men spoke from God as they were carried along by the Holy Spirit" (2 Pet. 1:21).

Peter says that God's Word did not come because human beings chose to give it; the Bible is not human speculation or human imagination. Would we humans be as honest as God was? We never would have revealed the clay feet of the great heroes of the Bible. We never would have shown David's failures, or Noah's drunkenness, or Lot's terrible plight. The Bible is realistic; it shows persons as they really are. We can look in the Word of God and see ourselves as in a mirror. It was written to deal comprehensively with human needs and to teach us the philosophy we need for life. It was written to clarify for us the true areas of reality. It was written to teach the right ethics by which people must live if they are to function according to the plan for which they were created. It was written to inform us of why we humans act as we do.

I have a friend in Texas who was a lineman for the telephone company. He lived a wild, reckless, purposeless life, and his marriage ended in divorce. He felt that no one wanted him, no one loved him. He was a disagreeable person who had made a mess of his whole life. He was in a hotel room in Abilene, Texas, contemplating suicide when he opened a Gideon Bible and saw in it the instruction "Plan of salvation, turn to these Scriptures." He began reading those Scriptures and within thirty minutes was on his knees saying: "God, I know You're alive. I know this Word is true. I know I'm a sinner. God, have mercy and forgive me and come into my life." The Lord did just what he asked Him to do, and now that man has changed his whole life, his whole nature. I know hundreds of people who have been changed by God's Word simply because they read it; because the Word of God is alive, vital, vibrant; and because it speaks to the needs of humankind.

When we claim that the Bible is inspired, there are some things we do not mean. For example, we do not mean that the Bible is inspired in the same sense that other great books or poems are inspired. Many inspiring works are the products of human genius. Such works contain profound and inspiring thoughts and ideas. This natural or human inspiration has great value, but the inspiration of the Bible is more than this. Neither do we refer to partial inspiration, the idea that some parts are inspired and others are not, when we speak of the Scriptures. Nor do we believe that the New Testament is more inspired than the Old Testament. Jesus brought insights and interpretations to the Old Testament that called for a new way of looking at it. A cardinal rule of biblical interpretation for Christians is that the Old Testament is interpreted by the New Testament. Still the Old Testament Scriptures, which were the only Bible the earliest Christians had, are recognized as equally inspired with the New

Testament writings. Finally, when we claim that the Bible is inspired, we do not mean that just its ideas are inspired but that its words are as well. We believe that writers were inspired in word and detail, as well as in ideas and concepts.

We often hear people speak of the original manuscripts of the Bible. The Christian world does not have any original manuscripts that the biblical writers themselves wrote. Careful and dedicated scholars over the centuries, however, have given us very ancient and completely dependable manuscripts. Very few words of the Bible are in question, and those that are make no difference to our faith and very little difference to our interpretation. Many excellent translations of the Bible are available. Regardless of the translation used, whether the 1611 King James Version or a contemporary one that takes into account the most recently discovered manuscripts, you can read most translations with complete confidence that you are reading the Word of God. All the good translations win the lost, speak to human needs, judge, teach, and bring us to a commitment to the Lord Jesus Christ.

The divine origin of the Bible is logical. That fact is based on the nature of God as a God who reveals Himself. Is it not reasonable that a revealing God would inspire a truthful, dependable, authoritative, inerrant record of His revelation? Would not a revealing God provide a standard against which we could measure right and wrong, perceptions about God, and the nature of redemption? Is it reasonable to believe that a revealing God would *not* provide an authoritative body of written material that could be studied to learn about Him, rather than leaving people to the whims of charlatans, unfounded mysticism, and sincere but wrong ideas? Indeed, it is completely illogical that a revealing God would *not* provide a written Word. These arguments testify to the divine origin of the Bible.

Jesus affirmed the Word of God in Matthew 22:29: "'You are in error because you do not know the Scriptures or the power of God.'" As a child in the Temple, Jesus confounded the scholars by His understanding of Scripture. During the temptation experience in the wilderness Jesus quoted and appealed to Scripture. He told His disciples, "'If you hold to my teaching, you are really my disciples. Then you will know the truth, and the truth will set you free'" (John 8:31-32).

God's Word: the Breath of God

The second truth of Hebrews 4:12 is that the Bible is "living and active." The word used in the King James Version is "quick." The Greek word is *zoa,* from which comes our word *zoology,* the study of life. *Zoa,* then, means *life.* The verse in 2 Timothy 3:16, quoted earlier, says that the Scriptures are "God-breathed." The Greek word for that phrase is *theopneustos. Theo* is *God,* and *pneustos* is *breathed.* All Scripture is God-breathed.

Genesis 2:7 sheds some light on this concept: "The Lord God formed man from the dust of the ground and breathed into his nostrils the breath of life, and man became a living being." God's inbreathing gave life to humankind. In the same way, God's in-breathing gives life to the written Word. It is not a book among books, not even if rated a classic. It is unique, for no other book is inbreathed by God. Writers often feel that they are inspired as they write. But that type of inspiration is not of the same nature as that of the biblical writers. God inspired them uniquely. But there is more: God breathed His breath into the written Word so that it is not just the inspired record of the writers; it is itself alive. The Bible breathes today, and it breathes the breath of God.

This living Word gives life. It delivers what it promises, and it promises to lead as we follow its precepts. It promises to be a lamp to our feet and a light to our paths (see Ps. 119:105). It promises to be dependable (see Ps. 19:7). It promises to correct and discipline (see Prov. 6:23). And it promises to guide us into real, abundant life as the Holy Spirit interacts with our spirits (see 2 Cor. 3:6). Jesus said: "'The Spirit gives life; the flesh counts for nothing. The words I have spoken to you are spirit and they are life'" (John 6:63).

Peter wrote, "You have been born again, not of perishable seed, but of imperishable, through the living and enduring word of God" (1 Pet. 1:23). Archaeologists once uncovered the tomb of a man of royalty. Among the treasures were a number of vases. Sealed with wax, they were found to contain seeds. Scientists decided to plant the seeds. To their amazement, the seeds sprouted. With water and sunlight those seeds, stored away for hundreds of years, produced life. That's the way God's Word is. When the water and light of a believing heart provide the soil for God's Word, life springs forth. You and I were saved because of that life-giving quality of God's Word.

God's Word: Indestructible
The third truth revealed about the Bible in Hebrews 4:12 is that it is "living and active. Sharper than any double-edged sword, it penetrates even to dividing soul and spirit, joints and marrow." Peter wrote that flesh is grass and passes away, "'but the word of the Lord stands forever'" (1 Pet. 1:25). Jesus said, "'Heaven and earth will pass away, but my words will never pass away'" (Matt. 24:35) and again, "'I tell you the truth, until heaven and earth disappear, not the smallest letter, not the least stroke of pen, will by any means disappear from the Law until everything is accomplished'" (Matt. 5:18). People have burned the Bible. They have burned its translators. They have made condensed versions of it, cutting out what they did not want. Nations and rulers have sought to eliminate it from their cultures and from the earth. Almost every home in America has a Bible. The Bible may be found in many languages all over the world. It exerts a powerful influence, even in places where non-Christian religions are dominant. The Bible, we must conclude, is under God's unique protection, and He is God of this universe.

God's Word is powerful; it will endure to the end of the age. It is a double-edged sword. One type of sword used in New Testament days was a short, pointed, double-edged sword like a double razor. It could cut in two directions. God's Word is like that in our lives. It is "edge all over." When you read it, it cuts into the soul and nature of the reader and of the hearer. When Peter preached on the Day of Pentecost, the people cried out under conviction, "'Brothers, what shall we do?'" (Acts 2:37). Even in the deep secrets of our hearts, God's Word penetrates. It convicts us to understand what is right and wrong. It reaches into the depths of our lives and gives us life by making us see ourselves as we really are and by awakening us to the powerful potential of what God calls us to be.

Revelation 19:13 pictures the return of Jesus at the end of the age. He is depicted in a robe dipped in blood, and from His mouth issues a sharp sword with which He will smite the nations. What is He called in that passage? The Word of God is His name.

God's Word: Convicting Power

Fourth, God's Word is a judging Word. Hebrews 4:12 says that God's Word "judges the thoughts and attitudes of the heart." The Greek word used in Hebrews 4:12, *kritikos*, appears in this form nowhere else in the Bible. Our word *critic* comes from this word. The Word of God peers into our lives, observes, judges, and determines what is right or wrong, good or bad, perfect or imperfect. It is a critic of our lives, the standard by which we are judged. A person might feel that when the time comes to stand before God in judgment, he can make the plea: "Lord, You understand. I am a twentieth-century man. I lived in the decade of the nineties. Those were times of changing morals. People were challenging the ethics of the Bible. You understand, don't You, Lord?" All the world must know that God will not judge on the basis of our family tree or the century in which we lived. He will judge on the basis of our faithfulness to the living Word.

John Quincy Adams called the attention of the United States Senate to two bushels. One bushel was from New York, the other from South Carolina. One bushel contained sixty-three more cubic inches than the other. Later that day he held in one hand a pound measurement from Maine and a pound measurement from Massachusetts. One pound weighed thirteen ounces more than the other. He asked the senators how this country could ever come together if bushels and pounds were measured differently. Produce could not be measured and weighed without confusion. Interstate commerce would be difficult. A bureau of weights and measures was established. A weighing machine with a circle around it is in the Smithsonian today. The machine is so sensitive that people must stand outside the circle lest the heat from their bodies affect the scale.

God has a scale, a measurement that is precisely accurate and that is the standard by which all else is measured. It is His Word. We will not be judged by any scale created by people, but by God's standard. It is our critic. God will judge us by it.

God's Word: Clear in Its Message

The Bible is clear in its message. Hebrews 4:2 reads, "We also have had the gospel preached to us, just as they did; but the message they heard was of no value to them, because those who heard did not combine it with faith." The gospel is not complicated. Most ethical issues are not complicated. The Bible's way of life is not complicated. Discipleship is not complicated. The message is muddled only when the mind and the heart are muddled. When people hear the Bible with an open and believing heart, its message is clear.

Peter cautioned that we must take heed to the Scripture, "as to a light shining in a dark place" (2 Pet. 1:19). Darkness is everywhere on this earth. The only truth you and I can depend on for certain is the Word of God. Its light shines into the lives and culture even of tribes in the darkest places of the earth.

Most evangelical Christians have heard the story of the Auca Indians, who killed the missionaries who took the gospel to them. Yet today the story is told in book and film about the Aucas' conversion, what God has done in their lives, and how the light of God's Word has made a difference. That is what God has done with His Word throughout the whole world.

Some people obscure the Bible's clarity, claiming that it contains contradictions and inconsistencies. That view is to be rejected. There is progression in the Bible, as God prepared Israel and the world for the coming of Jesus Christ, but the Bible is a whole. There is unity in the Bible. Baptists from our very beginning have claimed to believe in all of the Scriptures. All of the Bible is necessary for us to understand all of God that He has chosen to reveal to us. Paul instructed Timothy, "Do your best to present yourself to God as one approved, a workman who does not need to be ashamed and who correctly handles the word of truth" (2 Tim. 2:15). Second Peter 1:20 warns us of private interpretations. Some people construct their own theology by "cutting and pasting" verses of the Bible. This kind of slipshod study of the Word of God is nothing more than private interpretation. It is not correctly handling the Word of Truth but rather butchering the Bible, reconstructing it to suit our own fancies.

My father's business partner, who was not a Christian, had a heart attack and was near death. I had the chance to share with him the plan of salvation. Later, he called me back into the room; and before he died, he accepted Christ as his Savior. His wife asked me to preach his funeral to fulfill her husband's request. A Jehovah's Witness, she asked whether I would be willing to use the Scriptures she would suggest. I said I would if they were from the Bible. She later handed me a long list of texts, but they were fragments of texts that read quite differently when taken out of context. Of course, when I conducted the funeral service, I used the full texts. Satan often misuses the Scripture by fragmenting it, taking verses out of context so that they are distorted and misleading.

The Bible is historically unified. Although it was written over a period of many centuries, its message is historically logical and progressive. World religions generally see history as cyclical in nature. That is, history repeats itself in a continuous cycle over and over again. A nation rises, becomes powerful, decays, and is replaced by another nation, with history having no direction or purpose. Or a person passes through one incarnation after another on his possibly unsuccessful journey to Nirvana, the place of Buddhist bliss. Although we learn from history, a certain hopelessness arises from the view that nothing ever really changes as history moves through its cycles. The Christian view of history pictures it as a line rather than a circle, moving absolutely toward the climax that God intends for it. History had a beginning and will have an end. The Bible reflects this historical unity as it tells how God has revealed Himself and His will over a very long period of time. Moreover, we know, because the Bible tells us so, that God has a goal, a destiny toward which history moves. And as we study God's Word, we begin to see our individual places in that destiny, so the Bible reveals to us the incredible joy that we are part of what God is doing. We are sharing in eternal work. The diversity of the Bible is unified in this message. Its history, poetry, biography, proverbs, sermons, and theology all share in that unity.

When Dr. B. H. Carroll, dean of the Bible Department at Baylor University and first president of Southwestern Baptist Theological Seminary, was a young man, he thought he had found a thousand contradictions in the Bible. After he spent time in study, he realized that there were no contradictions. He had resolved all but six of them. He went on to admit, "I am disposed to think that if I had more sense I could harmonize those other six."[2] The Word of God is a unity. It does not break up or show disharmony. The Word of God has harmonious, factual understanding. It has theological unity. The themes of the covenants, the kingdom, grace, salvation, the coming of Jesus, and the second coming of Jesus move toward a historical end when Jesus is going to come again.

God's Word: the Believer's Authority

Some who have thought that the Bible was not clear enough have developed creeds. John Leland, a Baptist pastor who heavily influenced the writing of religious freedom into the Constitution, advised that the minute we develop a creed, we will have developed a cult that will stand between us and God. Therefore, he said, there should be one creed in Baptist life, the Word of God, and no other. That advice was wise in those days and is wise today. Truth and freedom are in the Word of God. Our Baptist forebears believed that and gave their lives to the concept that every person has the right to go to the Word of God for himself or herself. They insisted that people need no mediator, whether a priest or someone with a great education, to teach them the Word of God. Only the Holy Spirit can make that Word come alive.

John Wesley, the great evangelist and theologian of Christian history who was the father of Methodism, wrote: "I want to know one thing, the way to heaven—how to land safe on that happy shore. God himself has condescended to teach the way: for this very end he came from heaven. He hath written it down in a book. O give me that book! At any price give me the Book of God! I have it. Here is knowledge enough for me. Let me be

homo unius libri [a man of one book]."[3] A hymn writer expressed
a similar thought about the Bible.

O Word of God Incarnate, O Wisdom from on high,
O Truth unchanged, unchanging, O Light of our dark sky:
We praise thee for the radiance That from the hallowed page,
A lantern to our footsteps, Shines on from age to age.

—William W. How

The Bible is God's Book. It is divine, authoritative, infallible,
inerrant, God-breathed, and truth without mixture of error.

PERSONAL LEARNING ACTIVITY 1

Match the Bible verses or portions of verses with the correct references.

Bible Verses	References
1. ____ " 'Heaven and earth will pass away, but my words will never pass away.' "	*a.* 2 Timothy 3:16
2. ____ " 'The words I have spoken to you are spirit and they are life.' "	*b.* 2 Peter 1:21
3. ____ "All Scripture is God-breathed."	*c.* John 8:32
4. ____ "Men spoke from God as they were carried along by the Holy Spirit."	*d.* John 6:63
5. ____ " 'Then you will know the truth, and the truth will set you free.' "	*e.* Matthew 24:35

Answers: 1. *e*, 2. *d*, 3. *a*, 4. *b*, 5. *c*.

1. Tal D. Bonham, *Humor: God's Gift* (Nashville: Broadman Press, 1988), 73-74.
2. B. H. Carroll, *Inspiration of the Bible* (New York: Fleming H. Revell Company, 1930), 121.
3. John Wesley, *The Works of John Wesley*, ed. Albert C. Outler, vol. 1, *Sermons I, 1–33* (Nashville: Abingdon Press, 1984), 105. Used by permission.

CHAPTER 2

The Doctrine of God

God said to Moses, "I am who I am."
Exodus 3:14

GOD IS INFINITE AND PERFECT Spirit, a Person, who created and sustains the universe and all in it. He is actively involved in history and in persons to bring the world to the destiny He planned for it from the beginning.

We will consider various details of this definition: (1) God is One; (2) He is Spirit; (3) He is Person; (4) He is infinite; (5) He is perfect; (6) He is Creator; and (7) He moves history toward the destiny He planned. As we shall see, these details involve all the persons of the Trinity.

The One God: God Is One

When the Moslems swept over the Middle and Near East in the seventh century, they ruthlessly destroyed everyone whom they did not consider to be monotheistic in belief. They offered conquered people a choice to become Moslems or to be killed. Jews were allowed to live and to pursue their own religion because Moslems understood their religion to be the worship of the one God. All pagans—believers in more than one God—were slaughtered if they did not convert to Islam. Christians were considered to be pagans, for they could not make the Moslems understand that they were monotheists. The Christian belief in the Trinity seemed to the Moslems to be a belief in three Gods.

Mistaken ideas about the Trinity. In grappling with this doctrine, the Christian community has rejected a number of explanations over the centuries. A brief survey will help us understand the Trinity by clarifying what it is *not*.

First, the Trinity is not a succession of ways God has appeared in history. That is, God did not manifest Himself only as Father during the Old Testament period, only as Jesus the Son during the New Testament period, and only as Holy Spirit after Jesus' ascension. Such a view reduces the Persons of the Trinity to manifestations and denies the eternal nature of all three. This view sometimes is called modalism, meaning that God appeared in various modes at different times.

Second, the Trinity is not comprised of three Gods. This concept, called tritheism, sees the Trinity as three equal but separate Beings who make up a cooperative Godhead whose members confer as necessary.

Third, Jesus did not become part of the Trinity at some point in His life. This view holds that the human Jesus was adopted by the Father, usually at His baptism, at which time He was made divine. Called adoptionism, this concept maintains that the Holy Spirit conferred divinity on Jesus when the Spirit descended in the form of a dove.

An explanation of the Trinity. The word *Trinity* cannot be found in the Bible. Rather, the Christian belief in the Trinity is a way to understand what the Bible teaches about God. God is revealed in the Bible as Father, Son, and Holy Spirit. The word *Trinity* is a theological word used to describe this revelation.

The Trinity is a doctrine difficult to explain, even to Christians. It is a mystery known only to God Himself, and the Christian accepts it because the Bible teaches it, not because it can be rationalized.

When we think of God the Father, we identify Him as the God of the Old Testament and the One to whom Jesus prayed. The Father is the One we think of when we describe God's nature and discuss His characteristics. He is the One we refer to, then, when we speak of God.

Although we traditionally consider God's characteristics around the person of Father, Father is much more a New Testament concept than an Old Testament idea. *Father* is seldom used for God in the Old Testament, and each time the use is corporate, God being the Father of Israel the nation or people; never is *Father* used in the Old Testament to refer to an individual personal relationship.

The Gospels alone, on the other hand, contain more than 170 references to God as Father both in Jesus' references to His unique relationship as His Father's only begotten Son and in references to believers calling God Father, as in the Model Prayer. Thus, the Trinity appears more fully in the New Testament, even though all three Persons appear in the Old Testament.

The first appearance of the Holy Spirit is in Genesis 1:2: "the Spirit of God was hovering over the waters." References to the Son appear in the many messianic texts, and the New Testament insists that Jesus was the agent of creation (see John 1:3). Thus, all three Persons existed from eternity and were present at the creation.

Key biblical texts that mention all three Persons of the Trinity are Matthew 3:13-17; Romans 8:9; and Ephesians 1:17. Many other texts mention two Persons of the Trinity (Matt. 18:19-20; John 14:16; Acts 5:3-4; Rom. 9:5; 1 Cor. 12:3; 2 Cor. 3:17-18; Eph. 1:3). Christians came to the doctrine, then, because the Bible demands it; some doctrine must at least attempt to grapple with the facts that all three—Father, Son, and Holy Spirit—are called God and that all three Persons are used interchangeably for one another in various texts.

The only doctrine of the Trinity that will stand biblical tests is the view that God is One and has made Himself known as three eternal Persons. The Father, Son, and Spirit are a unity in a single Person. The concept cannot be completely understood by the human mind, and the use of *Person* to designate each of the three is confusing. However, no theologian throughout Christian history has come up with an adequate term, and so *Person* has been accepted as the best word.

By referring to each—Father, Son, and Holy Spirit—as Person, we emphasize that each is indeed a Person with personality and personal characteristics. However, we must not allow our minds to conclude that since they are distinct Persons, they are not one Person. Christians are monotheistic. Even though the doctrine of the Trinity is beyond our comprehension, we accept it as God's way of revealing Himself to us.

God revealed as Father, Son, and Holy Spirit. As indicated earlier, Father basically is a New Testament concept. When Jesus came, God was perceived to be so austere and removed in His holiness that even His name could not be spoken. When the Hebrew came to God's name in a text, he simply passed over it in silence. In time, God was referred to as "the name." Jesus, in clear and intentional contrast, taught His disciples to pray, "Our Father." This new relationship of Father and child became part of the evangelistic message of the early Christians, so much so that the word Jesus used, *Abba,* was used even with Greek-speaking converts (Rom. 8:15; Gal. 4:6). In fact, *Father* is not an accurate translation; *Abba* is an endearing, familiar term like our word *daddy.* We are not free to be flippant in our relationship; there is no place for a kind of "man upstairs" comradery. But we are free to "approach the throne of grace with confidence" (Heb. 4:16).

When we speak of Jesus as God's Son, we do not mean that God created Jesus at any point in time. Jesus always has existed, for He is God; there is no God apart from Jesus and no Jesus apart from God.

The Spirit is the third Person of the Godhead, and, like the first and second Persons, He is eternal. He is referred to occasionally in the Old Testament, and during later Old Testament times His coming in great power began to be prophesied. He was involved in Jesus' birth and present at various points in Jesus' ministry. The Day of Pentecost marked the fulfillment of Old Testament prophecies of the coming of the Holy Spirit in His fullness.

The One God: God Is Spirit

The definition of *God* given previously includes a reference to Him as Spirit. Jesus told the woman at the well that "'God is spirit, and his worshipers must worship in spirit and in truth'" (John 4:24). The very basis of the second commandment is that God cannot be depicted: "'You shall not make for yourself an idol in the form of anything in heaven above or on the earth beneath or in the waters below'" (Ex. 20:4). Baptists and most Protestants have insisted that any such aids to worship as saints, statues, or relics are not aids but limits to a person's concept of God. God is too great to be depicted. The only depiction that has been seen with human eyes is Jesus, God incarnate. A glance at the paintings and statuary of God and of Jesus throughout Christian history demonstrates how thoroughly artists depict God or Jesus in terms of their own finite minds: a God with angry eye and flowing beard, an effete Jesus, or in more recent times a Jesus with a Madison Avenue gaze. Such paintings and sculptures have their place in art but not in worship. God is spirit. His majesty cannot be described. He is in time and beyond time, in His creation and beyond it, immensely greater than history but involved in it.

The Old Testament often refers to God in human terms, a practice called anthropomorphic by scholars, meaning *in the form of man*. The Bible refers to God's finger (Ex. 31:18), His footstool (1 Chron. 28:2), His arm (Num. 11:23), His face (Num. 6:25), His eyes (2 Chron. 16:9), and His hand (Ps. 37:24), to list but a few. These references are poetic or picturesque ways of speaking of God and do not mean that some parts of the Bible teach that He is physical while other parts teach that He is spirit.

The One God: God Is Person

The next noun in our definition is *Person*, a word already discussed in regard to the Trinity but one that needs elaboration in terms of the Godhead. The Bible presents God as a Person when it discusses or assumes His behavior as a Person. He is conscious of Himself; He exercises thought and feeling; and He makes decisions. He is free; He relates to us in a personal way; and He acts in history. All of these characteristics are those of persons, not things or mystical concepts. God created humankind in His image; thus, if we are persons, He must be a Person.

good (

The Bible records many names of God. The most common Old Testament name is *Elohim*. Usually translated *God*, it first appears in Genesis 1:1. It is a general word, similar to our word *god*, which we use without the capital letter for false gods. This word is used in combination with various other words to describe characteristics or powers of God: *El Shaddai* means *God Almighty*, *El Elyon* means *most high God*, *El Olam* means *everlasting God*, *El Roi* means *God who sees me*. God was also called Lord many times in both Testaments.

God used a distinctive name, *Yahweh*, meaning *I Am*, to reveal Himself to Moses, a name that reveals much to us about God. This word also is used in combination with other words to make various statements about God, but the word itself is the root of the verb *to be*. Scholars have debated the exact meaning of the form of the name God gave Moses in Exodus 3:14, "I am who I am." With the verb *to be*, God was stating that He is the God who exists and always will exist and that He is the source of all that exists.

The One God: God Is Infinite

God's infinite nature can be described in five words: *eternal, immutable, omnipresent, omniscient,* and *omnipotent*.

God is eternal. God has always existed; there has never been a time when He did not exist. Since humans think in terms of time, they cannot fully grasp this concept. We must remember that God created time just as He created everything else. Somehow, He is above and beyond time. As we think of eternity, God stretches backward beyond the creation of the universe in a never-ending line. He was not created; if He were, He could not be the eternal God. God stretches beyond time as far as He stretches before it, in a never-ending line of existence. God will never cease to be. *Infinite* means *unlimited*, and God's existence is unlimited.

God is immutable. The word means unchanging. God is the same yesterday, tomorrow, and forever (see Ps. 102:27; Heb. 13:8). This concept is confusing to some as they consider texts that indicate that God "repented." At least thirteen times the Old Testament pictures God as changing His mind (Ex. 32:14; Deut. 9:19; 1 Sam. 15:11; 2 Sam. 24:16; 1 Kings 21:29; 1 Chron. 21:15; Ps. 106:45; Jer. 18:8; 26:3,19; Amos 7:3,6; Jonah 3:10). All of these texts describe God as changing His course of action in response to attitudes or actions of people. Never did God change His direction, alter His goal, violate His holiness or grace, or act capriciously. In fact, we can have confidence in God because He will, for example, withhold promised judgment if people repent. God's immutability guarantees that He will save as He promised He would; He will punish sin as He promised He would; He will move this world toward the destiny He planned for it before the beginning of time. His nature never changes.

God is omnipresent. This word means that God is everywhere at all times. There is never a time when His presence does not extend to all that is. The psalmist wrote: "Where can I go from your Spirit? Where can I flee from your presence? If I go up to the heavens, you are there; if I make my bed in the depths, you are there. If I rise on the wings of the dawn, if I settle on the far side of the sea, even there your hand will guide me, your right hand will hold me fast" (Ps. 139:7-10). This truth about God is both a warning to those who feel that they can escape God's presence and a promise to those who seek God's help. Wherever we are, at any time, God is there. Elijah chided the Baal prophets that their god perhaps had gone on a journey, and so they would have to wait until he returned before he would hear their prayers. Not so with Elijah's God. All of the "journeys" taken by our God do not diminish His presence in all the other places.

God is omniscient. This word means that God is all-knowing. There is nothing that He does not know. His insight pierces to the inner heart of every person everywhere simultaneously. The full range of scientific knowledge is known to Him. As humans begin to feel that they have outgrown God, that science has made God unnecessary, they would do well to compare their knowledge with God's. They will never outstrip Him in knowledge. This tremendous truth should cause every believer to turn his or her life over to God since He knows us better than we know ourselves. Paul urged us to test God's will for our lives, and we will approve the results; we will find that God's will is good, pleasing, and perfect (see Rom. 12:2).

God is omnipotent. God is all-powerful. No force, physical or spiritual, holds more power than God. The Bible teaches that God has *all* power. Any power Satan or an evil ruler has is held because God allows it. Jesus' disciples stood on a hill and watched Jesus ascend to the Father. His bodily presence had left them. They faced a hostile, unbelieving, persecuting, confused, power-hungry world in which Roman armies marched with iron armor and hobnailed boot. They remembered that Jesus had said, "'All authority in heaven and on earth has been given to me'" (Matt. 28:18). One day the trumpet will sound, and loud voices will proclaim from heaven: "'The kingdom of the world has become the kingdom of our Lord and of his Christ, and he will reign for ever and ever'" (Rev. 11:15). If you want to be on the power side, the winning side, be a disciple.

The One God: God Is Perfect

Our definition refers to God as perfect Spirit. The two words go together, for God could not be perfect if He were not spirit; to be otherwise would be too limiting. *Perfect* and *infinite* also go together, for together they cover much of God's nature and many of His characteristics. We shall consider under this heading some of God's characteristics, sometimes called moral attributes by theologians, who tend to list all of them under four: holiness, righteousness, truth, and love.

When we speak of holiness, we usually attach a rather harsh or sterile meaning to it. For example, one who lives a holy life is one who wears plain clothes and wears no makeup; or a holy thing is something used on an altar in a church; or a holy person lives above and beyond the call of duty. These views are shallow images of the biblical meaning of *holy*. Some Old Testament theologians claim that the Old Testament cannot be understood apart from a study of God as holy. The word *holy* has several uses in the Bible: (1) God's divine nature; (2) something set apart for God's use; and (3) moral qualities. In regard to God, His very nature is perfect holiness. The idea of being set apart refers to the priests and paraphernalia related to the temple and priestly work. Holiness in the sense of moral qualities is built on the first two in that true moral qualities reflect God's nature and are set-apart qualities. Leviticus repeats the admonition time and again to the people of God, "'"Be holy because I, the Lord your God, am holy"'" (Lev. 19:1), and this is commanded after a variety of instructions and commands not only for worship practices but also for social issues and personal sins. Life is to be lived by believers in ways that reflect whose we are. Our thoughts are to be set apart for God; our lives are to be holy sacrifices; our deeds are to be above reproach. God's holiness is absolute moral perfection, which is reflected in His dependability, love, grace, mercy, judgment, honor, and very being.

Righteousness is an attribute of God. This attribute means that God affirms right as opposed to wrong. He is righteous in that every one of His actions is right, and He has provided guidelines, such as commandments, for people to follow that help us to be righteous. His righteousness demands that He punish unrepentant evil; injustice will be judged. But His righteousness also is redemptive; for the righteous God has provided a way for unrighteous people (which includes all of us) to be redeemed, to be made righteous through the blood of Christ.

God is the source of all truth and is Himself ultimate Truth.
Nothing about God is untrue. The attribute of truthfulness refers to the unchanging absoluteness of God, but it also reflects the fact that full truth eludes us apart from God. Man is capable of discovering facts but is incapable of interpreting those facts adequately apart from God. No matter what realm of truth is being discussed—whether physical sciences, philosophy, or religion—it is grounded in God. Truth never contradicts truth. If we have problems with apparent facts and feel that they contradict the truth of God, the problem resides within us and not with truth. Truth in one field does not contradict truth in another field. The inquiring, believing mind will reconcile apparent contradictions through God's leadership, and the truth once thought to be contradictory will become a new window that lets in much brighter light than before.

God is love. God's love is the kind that seeks the best for those whom He created and does so at great cost to Himself. The Old Testament Book of Hosea tells the beautiful story of the love of Hosea for his unfaithful wife, Gomer. Hosea's love for Gomer was so strong and persistent that he did not give up on her, in spite of her unfaithfulness. This is a picture of God's love, even for the rebellious and ungrateful. The story of the prodigal son is also a picture of the Father's love. The Father rejoices in the salvation of a redeemed person no matter how ruthlessly that person treated Him earlier. The crucifixion of Jesus is the supreme demonstration of such love. God's love includes mercy and grace, without which we sinners would be doomed.

The One God: God Is Creator

The doctrine of God as creator is broader than His action in creating the universe. It includes His continuing work in sustaining that which He created, and it includes His involvement in His creation as He moves it toward the destiny for which He created it.

God is Creator of all. A strange reality becomes apparent when we attempt to discover God through His created order. Romans 1 points out that God has revealed enough of Himself through His creation that humankind should be able to discover Him through it; so obvious *should* God be in His creation that people are without excuse for not knowing and acknowledging God. The strangeness becomes apparent when we observe what people actually see when they seek to discover God through His creation. Instead of seeing God, they erect idols, or develop astrological charts, or worship the sun and moon, or celebrate the changing seasons with blatant fertility rituals. Even in the modern world people do not acknowledge God through a study of His creation but rather tend to worship the creation itself, becoming committed to a world view that denies or at least neutralizes anything God might have had to do with it. They, too, are without excuse.

All doctrine is intertwined; each subject bleeds over into others. Thus, as we study God as creator, we are reminded of the doctrine of depravity and of the doctrine of salvation. We become quite aware that people cannot—or will not—discover God apart from direct personal revelation by God of Himself to individuals.

The doctrine of God does not begin with creation and move back to an understanding of the God who created. Rather, an understanding of creation begins with the doctrine of God. We study God to learn more of His creation, rather than studying creation to discover God. To be sure, creation should inspire us to praise God for His wonderful works. God as creator, however, challenges us to ask questions such as: Why did God create this universe? Why did He create human beings in His own image and create them free? What purpose does God intend for this creation? How is God involved in it?

God created out of nothing. Baptists and other Christians debate *how* God created this universe. One absolute necessity of belief is that God created it out of nothingness (*ex nihilo*). If any raw material existed prior to the creation, then we must account for its creation. The biblical certainty is that God spoke and the creation came into existence, that speaking is all that was necessary, and that the creation would not have come into existence apart from God's speaking.

God is separate from His creation. Pantheism says that God exists in all things: A bit of God is in each tree, each cloud, each mountain and valley, each stream, and each flower. But the Bible sets God apart from His created order. The creation is not God, is no part of God. God does not need His creation; He exists independent of it.

God had a reason to create. Why, then, did God create a universe He did not need? In "The Creation" James Weldon Johnson, the black poet, has God speaking the simple line "I'm lonely" concerning the creation of humans. This simple statement is close to the mark, if it is not interpreted as meaning that a lonely God's needs could be satisfied only by creating something to give Him fellowship. God's reason for creation is tied to two attributes, His love and His glory. A parent does not need a child, but parents' lives are made richer by the presence of a loving child, a child who loves because he or she chooses to love. It is correct theology to say that God is enriched in His creation, though He does not *need* His creation. Protestant theologians generally have insisted that God created the universe ultimately to bring glory to Himself. That is an essential element in God's reason, but it must be seen in light of God's love. God is glorified as people willingly glorify Him, and that glorification of God by willing people will culminate in the new heaven and earth. Yet as people glorify God, they will reach their ultimate fulfillment and happiness. Their joy is clearly pictured in Revelation's description of heaven. An understanding of this reason why God created should undergird all of theology and all of life.

God sustains His creation. Colossians 1:17 asserts of Christ, "He is before all things, and in him all things hold together." Nehemiah 9:6 speaks of God's glorious acts in creation and adds, "And thou preservest them all" (KJV). Many other texts emphasize that this world could not continue to exist apart from God's sustaining it. This truth assumes some other important truths: (1) The energy or power that moves this universe has its source in God; (2) God is active in His creation; (3) the creation continues to be subject to God; and (4) God did not simply create the universe and then step apart from its functioning.

God the Sustainer is in control. God established this universe to operate according to certain rules, which might be called natural processes. The doctrinal term is concurrence. God cooperates with the natural processes that He Himself established. Two extreme, wrong positions violate this concept: (1) God never interferes with the natural laws He has established, and (2) God never uses the natural laws He established when He interjects His power into the physical world. In regard to the first, God is in control of His creation, and when He chooses to supersede or suspend natural law to cause a miracle, He can do so. No disbelief in miracles on the part of humans will alter God's power. He is in control of His creation; the creation has not taken control of itself from God. The second extreme is just as wrong. God is not flippant about the order that He created, and if natural laws can be used to bring about a miracle, it is no denial of miracles that God uses them. In fact, Exodus 14:21 clearly states that God used "a strong east wind" to turn back the waters.

God the Sustainer is involved in His creation. This logic is indisputable to a believer: (1) The universe would not exist had not God created it; (2) God would not have created the universe without a reason; and (3) God will be involved in the world to ensure that His reason is fulfilled. The doctrine of creation demands a long look at history. God is involved in history in any way He chooses to be. He may influence the natural order. He may influence the outcomes of battles or wars or politics. He may influence individuals' behavior. He may relate to believers in a special way. Books could be written on this point. How is God moving history toward the destination He planned for it? How does God change history? Under what conditions does God alter the natural flow of events? How does God work through unbelievers? How does God reveal His will to believers? How perfectly are believers capable of following the perfect will of God? "God is involved in His creation" is a profound truth with wide-ranging applications.

God moves this world toward a planned destiny. This concept, called Providence, involves God's foreknowledge and those strong arguments and feelings that once figured in Protestant and Baptist debates over predestination versus free will. God, before the foundation of the world, planned the world's destiny. He foreknew all that would happen and takes all of that into account in His work with this world. For the Christian, two important truths are illuminated by this concept: Christian hope is based on the absolute certainty that God will defeat all opposition and bring the world to its planned conclusion, and every believer has a place in working with God to accomplish that grand design.

The One God: God Is Sovereign

E. Y. Mullins's theological axiom in *The Axioms of Religion* is "The holy and loving God has a right to be sovereign."[1] His chapter deals with the way God's sovereignty expresses itself in His dealings with the world and the people He created and forms a basis for the priesthood of believers.

The sovereignty of God is another way of stating that God is in control. The concept needs attention, however, for an awareness of God's sovereignty is crucial for a proper understanding of God and humankind. Extreme predestination has caused some Christians to treat this concept rather lightly. Although some earlier Baptists (Particular) have been rigidly Calvinistic, Southern Baptists have been much too evangelistic to allow strict Calvinism to dominate their theology. This should demonstrate that belief in God's sovereignty does not result in extreme predestination. The priesthood of believers is a natural outgrowth of the sovereignty of God, for it claims that God does not delegate His sovereignty to any person or organization; God relates directly to the individual.

God's sovereignty is not objectionable if we assume that God is holy and loving; indeed, we want a God like that to direct our lives. The question remains, If God is sovereign, why doesn't He just make this world like He wants it and be done with it? Why drag it out? The answer lies in the fact that God created people to be free beings. To violate that freedom would short-circuit God's reason for creating people.

The sovereignty of God influences everything in the universe. He is sovereign over His created order. He is sovereign over every person. He is sovereign over every power. His sovereignty is ultimate and complete. All power that exists, exists because God allows it. He is sovereign over the believer and intends for the believer to acknowledge that sovereignty in loving obedience.

PERSONAL LEARNING ACTIVITY 2

A non-Christian friend asks you to explain how Christians can claim to believe in one God yet believe in the Trinity. Write how you would explain on the lines below.

_____

_____

_____

_____

_____

_____

1. E. Y. Mullins, *The Axioms of Religion* (Philadelphia: American Baptist Publication Society, 1908), 73.

CHAPTER 3

In God's Image

*Then God said, "Let us make man in our image, in
our likeness, and let them rule over the fish of the sea
and the birds of the air, over the livestock, over all
the earth, and over all the creatures that move along
the ground."*
Genesis 1:26

IN EARLIER TIMES THE BELIEF THAT
man was the crown and goal of creation was
not difficult to believe. Scientific discoveries bring an ever-
widening awareness of the immensity of the universe and shrink
humankind's image of itself. Many today claim that to believe
humans are the crown of creation or the center of the universe is
arrogant and naive.

In God's Image: Man the Goal of Creation

As we discovered in studying the doctrine of God, we do not
study the creation and extract from it our concept of God. God is
self-revealing. Due to our natures, we are incapable of knowing
God unless He reveals Himself to us. Thus, our view of God, His
world and purpose, and the nature of humankind should be
shaped not by our self-image—which changes with new discoveries or other successes and failures—but rather by revelation.

The biblical view is that humans are the crown of creation and
were God's goal in the creation. Rather than making us proud,
that fact should humble us and bring us to worship God in gratitude. When we gaze outward into the boundless sky, our awe
should bring forth grateful praise that God created all of it for us.
The issue of life on other planets or other uncertainties should

not concern the faith of believers. Whatever else exists does not change the nature of God, the truth God has given us about ourselves, or the way of salvation.

In God's Image: Persons, like God

The nature of personhood was discussed in the previous chapter. When God is compared to humans or humans are compared to God, we discover that we share many of the same characteristics. This is true even though God is infinite and humans are finite. God is spirit (see John 4:24). Humans are both physical and spiritual (see Gen. 2:7). In spite of these differences, humans share the characteristics of personhood with the Creator.

Both men and women were created in God's image. The medieval interpretation that God created man in His image, then created woman out of man's image, will not stand biblical scrutiny. Genesis 1:27 reads, "God created man in his own image, in the image of God he created him; male and female he created them." The word for *man* used here is *adam*, which means *mankind*, inclusive of both sexes. This text, properly interpreted, says that God created humankind in His own image and that both male and female reflect God's image.

To be created in the image of God and to be given the wonderful gift of personhood means that in many respects we are like God. Humans have intelligence and can think abstractly, qualities the animal world holds only in rudimentary fashion. We are able to be conscious of ourselves, to reason about persons and ideas. We have the ability to be rational in our commitments, while animals have only instinctive affection. This rational love allows us to choose to act out our love regardless of circumstances or responses. We have free will, the right to choose from a range of options and the right to be right or wrong. We also have a moral sense, a conscience; this characteristic is not an absolutely dependable source of ethics and action, but it is a characteristic that is unique to humans.

In God's Image: Persons Are a Unity

The unique combination of the physical and the spiritual in humans does not produce a dichotomy or trichotomy. That is, a person is a unitary being, made up of a body and soul—or body, soul, and spirit—not a soul that resides in a body (dichotomy). The Greek view, which still crops up occasionally, is that the soul is independent of the body; that is, the body is simply a house in which the soul resides. Therefore, the body may do as it pleases, for it has no effect on the soul. This view has its origins in ancient Greece. Some Greek philosophers exalted the soul and reason, teaching that the body is material and therefore evil. If the body is evil, it may be expected to act in evil ways; the soul is above the body and is not influenced by it.

This view influenced gnosticism, against which several of the New Testament writers argued. It may also have influenced the monastic movement, which encouraged fleeing the world and subjecting the body to various types of ascetic practices to bring the body under control.

Few people would deny that a person's body has an enormous shaping influence on the way one thinks about oneself, especially in relation to other people. A person who is physically small must learn ways to compensate for the lack of strength compared to large, muscular persons. A handsome man or a beautiful woman generally develops social skills that are quite different from those of the unattractive person. A case could be argued that in a perfect world this would not be the case, but the point is that the body and the mind cannot be separated; likewise, the soul cannot be separated from the body. Although the earthly body will be discarded, Paul pointed out that we will be given heavenly bodies (1 Cor. 15:35-44).

In God's Image: Persons Are Related

3 .

A major conclusion from the Genesis account of the creation of humankind is that all people of the earth have descended from common parents, who were created in the image of God. Any belief that sets one race above another directly conflicts with the clear teaching of Scripture. All persons are created in the image of God, and all persons are related to one another. The implications of this truth are enormous for evangelism and missions, relief efforts, strivings for peace, and every other context for relationships among people.

4.

In God's Image: Persons Have Potential

Persons have collective potential. When God created human-kind, He commanded the male and the female to fill the earth, subdue it, and rule over all creatures (Gen. 1:28). Human progress is the process of bringing that command to pass. Christians have sometimes been accused of using this text as a justification for abusing the resources of the earth. This is a false accusation. Christians are aware that subduing the earth means mastering the earth and using it as good stewards should for the good of all. The task of ecology is better served by those who believe that the created order belongs to God and must be treated with reverence and respect.

SELF-IMAGE:
BALANCED
WHOLESOME
POSITIVE

Persons also have individual potential. A subpoint in Walter Thomas Conner's *Revelation and God* is stated, *"The incarnation shows man's capacity for God."*[1] Jesus demonstrated how God intends for life to be lived. Sometimes the word *perfect* as used in the Bible means *complete* or *mature,* but we must not allow ourselves to miss the fact that God holds us accountable for perfect living; the fact that the presence of the sinful nature (Rom. 7) keeps us from becoming perfect does not lessen the requirement. The demand for perfection is implicit in numerous texts, such as the frequent repetition of "'"Be holy because I, the Lord your God, am holy"'" (Lev. 19:1) and the clear command "'Be perfect, therefore, as your heavenly Father is perfect'" (Matt. 5:48). This does not mean, "Be mature as your heavenly Father is mature." The goal of perfection is unattainable (Baptists do not believe in sinless perfection); yet that is the goal for which we are to strive.

Jesus' life provides the model for that striving; and the Holy Spirit provides the power and the leadership. A person's potential is enormous. Christians have for centuries believed that persons are sinful by nature and prone to sin when the opportunity arises, and in recent decades they have been accused of having a very low view of human nature. The accusation is true and false.

NOTE:

Christians indeed do have a low view of the potential of persons who do not know Christ, and history—including recent history—demonstrates the truth of that conclusion. But no one has a higher view of persons than do Christians for those who are redeemed. Even those religions that hold out divinity or near divinity for their followers do not hold as high a hope for redeemed persons as does the New Testament. No religion emphasizes the tremendous potential of life on this side of death as does Christianity. The promise of life is that God will guide every willing person to reach the highest potential in every area of life: interpersonal relationships, morality, judgment, wisdom, skills, contribution to society, fulfillment, and joy of life.

God has created human beings to be born again. Nine months go by to prepare an infant for physical birth. What a tragedy when birth does not occur! When persons live through this life and never know the new birth, they never become what God created them to be. People are born to be born again.

Many of the things that the world counts as praiseworthy are gladly released when a person meets Jesus in the experience of salvation. Paul discovered true wealth in Jesus. He threw his old value system onto the rubbish heap. He shed it like a cocoon and was set free in Christ. The German philosopher Nietzsche, in a bitter condemnation of what accepting Christ does in a person's life, called this the "'trans-valuation of all ancient values.'" He said that all the great manly virtues of power, aggression, and self-reliance were canceled out by the cross and its message of love, patience, humility, forgiveness, and grace.[2] Thank God he was right. When we meet Jesus at the cross, we become new persons.

In God's Image: Persons Are Created Free

FREEDOM / RESPONSIBILITY

The doctrine of the priesthood of believers is discussed in chapter 7; here it should be noted that the doctrine works backward from salvation to include freedom for every person. The more freedom is suppressed, the more society struggles in vain to solve its problems. Whenever freedom in matters of faith has been ignored and government or state-church views have been imposed on citizens, true faith has been replaced with religious trappings. God created persons in His image, and God is free. Baptists for four hundred years have insisted consistently that every person has the freedom to choose Christ or reject Him. The Constitutional clause that "all men are created equal" is a biblical creation concept.

This freedom, rightly developed in a person, results in his desire to be part of a community of free persons. It recognizes the equality of others in the community, and so free people together seek the good of all. Rightly understood, freedom results in servanthood ministry in mutual submission to one another, for the person truly and fully free in Jesus Christ yearns for others to enjoy that freedom and does all in her power to bring it to pass. It is no wonder that most missionaries in the world today are sent out by free churches.

Fallen in Sin: the Origin of Sin

No theologian or philosopher has been able to answer adequately the problem of evil and suffering. The Greek dichotomy called gnosticism developed among early Christians. This view claimed that the body was the origin of sin; when the body is destroyed, so is sin. Another erroneous view of sin's origin is that it is due to ignorance; education and culture eventually can eliminate sin. Others trace the origin of sin to Satan and feel that sin existed before the fall. Those who propose this view point to Jude 6; 2 Peter 2:4; and 1 John 3:8. The texts referred to certainly categorize Satan as a blatant sinner, but many scholars feel that the texts say no more than that. A more probable theory is that sin is a direct result of God's creating persons as free. Although Satan is ultimately responsible for sin, if people were not free, Satan would have no way to do his evil work. It was the misuse of freedom that led to humanity's fall. Without freedom—the right to decide to do right or wrong—sin could not have occurred.

Fallen in Sin: the Nature of Sin

Sin is universal. Many people who object to the term *total depravity* have no problem with the truth that sin is universal. Perhaps they react to the words more than to the concept, for the concepts actually have the same results. The universality of sin is a clear teaching of Scripture (Ps. 14:1-3; 51:5; Jer. 17:9; Luke 11:13; Rom. 3:9-18; Rom. 5:12-21; Eph. 2:3).

The Bible sums up the result of sin succinctly: "The wages of sin is death" (Rom. 6:23). Both physical and spiritual death are meant. As a direct result of the fall, Adam and Eve were told that they would die (Gen. 3:19). Sin resulted in separation from God, shame, guilt, disruption of personal relations, pain and suffering, loss of freedom, bondage to sin, and physical death.

Psalm 51 was written by David; yet it stands in stark contrast to the beautiful twenty-third Psalm. It is a psalm of deep, dark despair. How could one man write both psalms? The answer lies in the human experience of sin.

Psalm 51 reveals sin's effect. The psalm reflects the pain David had after his sin with Bathsheba, his arranging for the death of her husband, and the results of those awful sins. The first person affected, of course, is the one who commits the sin. David admitted to Nathan, "'I have sinned against the Lord'" (2 Sam. 12:13). He assumed full responsibility. He did not blame sin on his inheritance, on his ancestors, on his environment, on contemporary morality, on Bathsheba, or on Uriah. He admitted his own sin. David had allowed an awful sin to come into his life and rob him of joy in God. Sin wreaked havoc in his life and affected the life of each child born into his family. It ruined his heritage; it diminished the trust people had placed in him as a godly king; and it affected the devotion and love that his army had for him.

Sin soils the life of the sinner. David felt this burden so much *a.* that he cried out in verse 7 for God to purge him. He remembered what it was like to be clean, and he wanted God to restore that inner cleanness to him. David compared its loss to broken bones. Depression had replaced joy in his life.

Sin can affect the sinner physically. Some readers may recall a *b.* book published several years ago, *Whatever Became of Sin?* It had a message the world today wants to reject. Sin affects physical health. In Paul's discussion about partaking in the Lord's Supper (1 Cor. 11), he warned that some were doing so unworthily, and as a result, "That is why many among you are weak and sick, and a number of you have fallen asleep" (1 Cor. 11:30). Whatever else that phrase means, it surely means that sin exacts a large physical penalty. And the sin does not have to be one of the obvious health hazards—alcohol, drugs, or tobacco. Any kind of immorality, from adultery to ego problems, can affect us physically.

David wanted a clean heart, a right spirit. In his pride, he tried to cover up sin with his arrogance and his pride. As king, David literally got away with murder as well as adultery. But he found that such undisciplined use of power carries a heavy price tag. He cried out, "My sin is always before me" (Ps. 51:3), and he pleaded for God to free his spirit (v. 12).

C. Sin separates the sinner from God. David prayed in verse 11, "Do not cast me from your presence or take your Holy Spirit from me."

D. Sin silences a person's witness. David acknowledged that when he was forgiven, "then I will teach transgressors your ways, and sinners will turn back to you" (Ps. 51:13).

E. Sin affects God. In 2 Samuel 12:13, the text Psalm 51 is based on, David said, "'I have sinned against the Lord.'" He admitted it again in verse 4 of the psalm, and in that same verse he further indicated that he knew God would have to judge his sin. In effect, he said: "Lord, if you do not punish me, if you do not do something about this sin and immorality in my life, people are going to say you're not a just judge. Lord, it's not only my reputation that is on the line, but yours as well."

F. Sin affects other people. It made Bathsheba an object of lust. The child born to them died. Uriah was purposely sent to his death. David's son Absalom tried to unseat his father as king. Another son, Abner, raped his own sister and was killed for the act. Who is to say to what extent Israel's history was affected? Without a doubt, sin is no private matter. It is crucial to a nation's survival that its citizens live ethically. Isaiah 3:8 says: "Jerusalem staggers, Judah is falling; their words and deeds are against the Lord, defying his glorious presence."

A good study would be to track each of David's children to determine how David's sin affected them. Earlier Old Testament passages tell us that a person's sin is passed on to the third and fourth generations. Ezekiel spoke a new word that children could no longer blame their parents for their sins; he prophesied a gospel of individual accountability. That is the New Testament view as well. Even so, the experience remains that the sins of parents influence generations to come. God does not judge children for parents' sins, and parents' failures are no excuse for anyone to reject responsibility for his or her own actions. Yet an old sage wisely said that every person should choose his grandparents with care. No matter how merciful God is, if we go on in our sin, a chain reaction will be set off that will go into generation after generation.

Years ago a man was bird-watching on the Isle of Man. He watched an eagle swoop from the sky and snatch a small animal in its claws, soaring back up into the sky. The sight was magnificent, and the man watched enraptured through his binoculars. But then the eagle began to fly erratically, losing control, and finally plummeting to earth. The man felt sure that the eagle was dead, and he ran the great distance to where the eagle fell. He saw feathers everywhere, and soon he found the eagle. Stooping, he turned the eagle over and immediately realized what had happened. The eagle had caught a badger and had pulled the animal to its chest with its face toward its own chest. The badger had eaten at the eagle's very vitals all the way to the eagle's heart, but the eagle would not let it go.

"WAGES OF SIN"

Sin is like that. We pick it up and hold it to our breast until it destroys us, but we do not want to let it go.

Fallen in Sin: a Description of Sin

Several words and phrases describe human sin. A brief study of these will help us understand the human condition.

Warped conduct. Iniquity is the Hebrew word *aven*, which basically refers to something twisted or warped or crooked, thus a depravity of conduct. It is unholiness, defilement, a violation of the character of God. This concept of sin covers the entire gamut, because any sin is a violation of the command " " "Be holy because I, the Lord your God, am holy" " " (Lev. 19:1).

a.

Willful rebellion. Adam and Eve were guilty of this sin. They knew exactly what God had commanded about the forbidden fruit; yet they willfully chose to disobey. This sin is not ignorance of the law but rebellion in spite of knowing the law. One Greek word for this type of sin is translated *enmity*. It depicts a mind set against God or against another person or group. Through the cross, Christ broke down the enmity between persons and persons and between persons and God.

b.

This concept is close in meaning to rebellion, but the words used are different ones. It refers to overstepping boundaries, painting outside the lines established not by society but by God, and intentionally violating the law.

c. *Transgression.* This word is *pasha*, which means *unlawfulness or outlaw* or *willful rebellion*, setting up one's life and desires over against the will of God. Transgression is a violation of the boundaries that God has set. In the course of my ministry people have informed me that they intended to pursue their course of action regardless of what the Bible says.

d. *Missing the mark.* Another word usually translated *sin* is the Hebrew word *chata*. It means *to fall short of the mark*. God's law sets a target toward which we are to aim our lives, a target we miss when we sin. The word can refer to individual sins or to manner of life. A great human tragedy occurs when a person lives life outside God's plan.

e. *Unbelief.* The attitude of unbelief is the underlying cause of all sin. The word of the Holy Spirit includes convicting the world of sin, because the world does not believe in Christ (John 16:8-9).

Breach of covenant. God's covenant with Israel included both standard of living and mission. Continually, Israel was called to account because of covenant violations. Covert sin is not the only kind of sin; any loss of commitment to the mission to which God has called His people is sin. Loss of fellowship with God is another dimension of sinning against the covenant. The new covenant has God's law carved on the soft flesh of the heart (Jer. 31:34), and in it we call God Father. Ignoring this marvelous relationship is sin.

g. *Ungodliness.* This word indicates irreverence.

h. *Debauchery.* One New Testament word for *sin* means *debauchery, licentious living,* or *sensuality.*

i. *Depravity.* Depravity refers to a person's character, what he or she is, not just acts committed. Another Greek word closely connected in meaning has the idea of wickedness or maliciousness.

j. *Sin against God.* All of these words and others not listed help us understand the nature of sin, but the bottom line is that sin is rebellion against God and His revealed will. One of Paul's points in Romans 1 is that in spite of God's revealing much of Himself through the created order, humankind rebelled against the light and turned to awful and persistent sin. Many theologians have identified selfishness as the ground from which sin grows. People want more for themselves and want to control their own lives, and they act from selfish motivation regardless of the effect their lives have on others.

It is important to realize that God has not set up a list of do's and don'ts just to have some rules by which to test obedience. God gave His laws because He cares for everyone. Sometimes God's instructions do not appear reasonable to human reason. Once we have determined that the law is indeed God's and not some human addition, we are obligated to keep it. Obedience includes obeying just because God commands. A disregard of God's command because we think it is unnecessary or foolish or because the times have changed reflects an incredible arrogance on our part and a disregard of God's knowledge. *NOTE!*

Fallen in Sin: the Results of Sin

The fall refers to the event when Adam and Eve, who previously were sinless (innocent) and in close relationship with God, chose to disobey God and fell from a state of innocence to a sinful state.

The threefold appeal of the temptation has often been identified as the continuing nature of temptation: the desire for something good that God chose to withhold, the desire for something beautiful, and the desire to attain knowledge. I doubt that these three desires account for all sin, but they certainly are the pattern followed very often.

No matter how one catalogs the types of temptation represented in the fall, the essence of the sin was that Adam and Eve *decided* to act independently of God. Frank Stagg wrote: "It is the story of man's self-love, self-trust, and self-assertion. First came the doubt of God: Is God's will really good for us? Are God's commands binding? Cannot one manage for himself? Doubt became distrust and then disobedience."[3]

The term *original sin* is given to the doctrine that all humans since Adam and Eve have been born into sin. David cried out, "Surely I have been a sinner from birth, sinful from the time my mother conceived me" (Ps. 51:5). The concept has been ex-

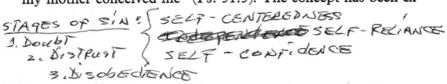

STAGES OF SIN: SELF-CENTEREDNESS
1. Doubt   INDEPENDENCE SELF-RELIANCE
   2. Distrust SELF-CONFIDENCE
      3. Disobedience

plained in various ways. Paul wrote, "Therefore, just as sin entered the world through one man, and death through sin, and in this way death came to all men, because all sinned" (Rom. 5:12).

The doctrine of original sin gave rise to the idea of infant baptism. At the earliest possible moment, the infant's sin had to be washed away lest the child die and go to hell. (Some Reformers reinterpreted infant baptism to be entry into the Christian community, comparable to Old Testament circumcision.)

INNOCENT
"SAFE"

AT OF
ACCOUNT-
ABILITY
SAVED/
LOST

Baptists believe in original sin but insist that no one goes to hell simply on the basis of inherited sin. Baptists hold that responsibility for one's sin comes at the age of accountability, meaning that God does not hold persons accountable for their sin until they reach the age when they become conscious of the difference between right and wrong, an age that differs with different people.

The term *total depravity*, which came from Calvinism, is still used by many Baptists. It means that all persons are born with a propensity to sin. It is directly connected with original sin but generally allows for various explanations of how original sin persists in the human race. For example, some writers insist on some kind of physical or spiritual characteristic that has been passed on somehow from generation to generation ever since Adam. Other writers feel that an evil society guarantees that all born into it will become evil. The important point is not the method of transmission. The question is whether humans have a sinful nature that will result in sin or whether humans must be punished because they are sinners by nature. The latter view holds that somehow all Adam's descendants are held accountable for *his* sin; some say that every descendant of Adam was somehow present and so participated in his sin and must be punished for it, a view called Federalism.

Total depravity is an easy term to understand. It does not mean that everyone born is as evil as he or she can become, or that the sinner can do no good, or that the sinner has no knowledge of God. It means, rather, that humans are basically and inherently prone to do wrong rather than right. Humanism, for example, generally holds the opposite view, that people are basically and inherently good and will do good, given a reasonable chance to do so. Obviously, which of the two views of humankind a person holds makes a great deal of difference in how he goes about dealing with the wrongs of a society and how he evangelizes.

Satan: the Enemy of Humankind

Satan is a personal, evil force in command of the sin of this world. Believing in Satan and attributing such control to him do not lessen human responsibility for sin. We cannot flippantly ignore the consequences of sin by joking, "The devil made me do it." We are told quite clearly to resist Satan, and we are given the power to do so (see Jas. 1:13-16).

In the New Testament Satan is referred to as Satan, the accuser, the tempter, the destroyer, the evil one, the enemy, the old serpent, the prince of the world, Beelzebub, and Belial; and he is called by various types of sin such as liar and murderer. He is shown as responsible for sin and, through demons, being responsible for causing disease, disability, unbalanced behavior, and death.

The Book of Revelation gives Satan a prominent place and reveals how fully sin has its source in him. He does all he can to delude believers as well as others. But one day he will be destroyed. He is not in control of this world, even though he sometimes seems to be; God is.

PERSONAL LEARNING ACTIVITY 3

Read the statements below and circle *T* for those that are true and *F* for those that are false.

T F 1. The biblical view is that humans are the crown of creation.

T F 2. Man is created in God's image, but woman is created in man's image.

T F 3. The soul is independent of the body; therefore, what the body does has no effect on the soul.

T F 4. A person is a unitary being, made up of body, soul, and spirit.

T F   5. Any belief that sets one race above another conflicts with the teachings of Scripture.

T F   6. God's command for man and woman to rule over the earth and subdue it gives us permission to use the earth in any way we wish.

T F   7. Ecology is a concern of those who believe that the created order belongs to God.

T F   8. Baptists have consistently defended the individual's right to choose Christ or reject Him.

T F   9. Belief in original sin does not mean believing that a person is lost because of inherited sin.

T F 10. Since Satan is a personal evil force in the world, people are not responsible for their sin.

Answers: 1. *T*, 2. *F*, 3. *F*, 4. *T*, 5. *T*, 6. *F*, 7. *T*, 8. *T*, 9. *T*, 10. *F*

1. Walter Thomas Conner, *Revelation and God* (Nashville: Broadman Press, 1936), 53.
2. Paul S. Rees, *The Adequate Man: Paul in Philippians* (Westwood, New Jersey: Fleming H. Revell Company, 1959), 71.
3. Frank Stagg, *New Testament Theology* (Nashville: Broadman Press, 1962), 19.

CHAPTER 4

The Doctrine of Christ

*In the past God spoke to our forefathers through the
prophets at many times and in various ways, but in
these last days he has spoken to us by his Son, whom
he appointed heir of all things, and through whom he
made the universe. The Son is the radiance of God's
glory and the exact representation of his being,
sustaining all things by his powerful word. After he
had provided purification for sins, he sat down at the
right hand of the Majesty in heaven.*
Hebrews 1:1-3

A ROMAN WRITER NAMED PLINY
prayed: "Oh, God, won't you show us what
you intended the world to be? Won't you show us some way what
purpose you had for us? Could not you give us a perfect example?" Hebrews 1:1-3 answers Pliny's question. It tells us that
God spoke in times past in many ways but that His last word is
Jesus. This passage tells us that God appointed Jesus to be heir of
all things. It says that Jesus made the universe. It tells us that
Jesus is the exact representation of the being of God. It tells us
that Jesus provided purification for sins and sat down at God's
right hand. Peter tells us that this was God's plan from the beginning: "He was chosen before the creation of the world, but was
revealed in these last times for your sake" (1 Pet. 1:20).

Previous revelations of God were fragmented. God has spoken
in many ways, and in all of the ways God spoke, He was preparing the world to hear His final word. The Hebrew text uses two
figures to emphasize that Jesus is the perfect revelation of God.

First, Jesus is "the radiance of God's glory" (Heb. 1:3). He is
the shining glory of God. As light shines from the sun, Jesus
radiates God. When Jewish scholars spoke of God's radiant glory,
they often used the Hebrew word *shekinah*. That intense pres-

ence of God was in the cloud by day and the fire by night and led the Hebrews from the wilderness. It was the brightness that glowed in Moses' face when he came down from the mountain, so bright that Moses had to cover his face with a veil. But its most concentrated presence was in the holy of holies, on the mercy seat, which was the lid of the ark of the covenant. That same *shekinah* glory was present in the transfiguration of Jesus. Jesus is that intense presence of God, that shining radiance of the Godhead.

Jesus: the Incarnation of God

Incarnation as it refers to Jesus means *God in the flesh*. Even before He created the world, God decided that He would come down to this earth and live in the world He had created. He would come as a newborn baby, born into a human family. He would live in poverty in a simple home. He would live in a time when the Jewish people would be under the power of the Roman Empire. He would be tempted in every way humans can be tempted; yet He would live a perfect life, demonstrating in word and deed how people should live. For three years He would walk through the little country of Judea and tell everyone about the love of God. Finally, He would demonstrate the love of God by dying on the cross as a substitute for all who would believe. He would conquer death and sin by rising from the dead.

Paul spoke of the incarnation when he wrote, "Your attitude should be the same as that of Christ Jesus: who, being in very nature God, did not consider equality with God something to be grasped, but made himself nothing, taking the very nature of a servant, being made in human likeness" (Phil. 2:5-7). Jesus limited Himself in order to accomplish the work of redemption.

Jesus created the universe. Jesus was the agent of creation (see John 1:1-3; Heb. 1:10). He was not a newly created expression of God when He came to earth as a baby. He was the Person of the Godhead who created the universe and all that exists. Jesus is God, and He made each of us, so He knows us better than anyone else. He made each of us unique individuals. All of our differences are known to Him. That is a comforting thought: He knows us, and still He loves us.

Jesus is eternal. He will never change (see Heb. 1:11–12). The world moves toward its inevitable end. Material things wear out, and fashions change. Even religion changes. But Jesus does not change. He is the same yesterday, today, and forever (see Heb. 13:8). The four Gospels reveal Jesus as one who loved people and had compassion for them. He does not change. He still relates to the needs of people with caring and mercy.

Jesus: Born of a Virgin

Two of the four Gospels (Matthew and Luke) relate the virgin birth of Jesus, describing it in some detail. John assumes it (see John 1:14), as does Paul (see Gal. 4:4). Those references are enough to guarantee belief in the virgin birth of Jesus by believers who accept the Bible as God's inspired Word.

Some with a more liberal theology question the virgin birth. Once this biblical truth is denied, the next step for some is to deny Christ's divinity. Belief in the virgin birth is absolutely essential to normative Christianity. When people are first saved, sometimes they know nothing about the virgin birth of Jesus. Some simply have not heard; others are too young to know what it means. However, as a person comes to terms with Jesus as divine and the Bible as the authority, a denial of the virgin birth rejects the biblical teachings about Jesus. Such a denial may lead to an increasing disbelief in other biblical truths. The Bible clearly teaches that God is Jesus' Father, that He was conceived by the Holy Spirit (Matt. 1:18). This doctrine of the virgin birth of Jesus is important. It affirms that Jesus is uniquely the Son of God.

Jesus: the Supreme Revelation

The first test of a false cult is what it teaches about Jesus. Many of these cults hold to an unbiblical view of Christ. They believe that some other revelation has superseded that given by Jesus. Whatever claims a cult may make about its commitment to Jesus, if He is not given first place as the final and complete revelation of God, its teaching is false.

We ask of a cult a key question, What do you believe about Jesus? Any group claiming that some additional revelation has come after Jesus is a cult, for God chose to reveal Himself finally and *fully* in Jesus. Hebrews emphasizes that Jesus is the perfect revelation of God. Paul wrote, "In Christ all the fullness of the Deity lives in bodily form" (Col. 2:9).

Jesus said, "'I am the way and the truth and the life. No one comes to the Father except through me'" (John 14:6). Philip said, "'Lord, show us the Father and that will be enough for us'" (John 14:8). Jesus responded in the next verse, "'Don't you know me, Philip, even after I have been among you such a long time?'" The teaching is clear. Anyone who has seen Jesus has seen the Father. The long search for God is unnecessary, for He is here in Jesus Christ and nowhere else. To see the glory of God, look to Jesus. To experience the forgiveness of God, look to Jesus. To know the healing of God, look to Jesus. To learn how God cares, look to Jesus. To enter God's kingdom, look to Jesus. To study the nature of God, look to Jesus.

Jesus is "the exact representation of his being" (Heb. 1:3). Jesus is God's portrait. The Greek word is *charakter,* from which comes our word *character.* One of the communication techniques used by rulers in the first century was to imprint on coins and statues a message along with a personal image. If an emperor wanted an image of generosity, he stamped his image on one side of a coin and a deity known for generosity on the other side. He raised statues all over the empire depicting himself as he wanted people to know him. The readers of Hebrews were familiar with images selected to communicate the characteristics of the ruler. Jesus is the express image of God. He communicates perfectly what God wants us to know of Him.

One reason Baptists do not believe in images is because no human creation can improve on Jesus' picture of God. Any attempt to do so brings God down rather than exalting Him. These statues constructed by humans are not aids to worship; rather, they focus our eyes on the object rather than on Jesus, who is the only image of God we should study. We do not find God pictured in His servants, no matter how mighty they may be in pulpit or leadership skills. We do not find God truly represented in paintings or statues. We find God only in Jesus Christ.

John 1:1 calls Jesus the Word. He is the statement of God, the final and complete statement that never will be superseded. When you hear a word, it calls an idea to your mind. Words such as *ice, fire, daughter, grandson,* and *paycheck* bring clear concepts to your mind. When we hear the name *Jesus,* the reality of God's nature comes to mind.

Jesus: Prophet, Priest, and King

Jesus came to this earth to complete a threefold work as a prophet, priest, and king. As a prophet, Jesus reveals and announces God to humankind. Jesus' work as a prophet included teaching His disciples that He is the way, the truth, and the life (see John 14:6). His miracles and parables alike are filled with moral meaning. He constantly led His disciples to a higher understanding of the kingdom of God. He personified truth in every act of His life: in the deeds He did, the words He spoke, and the giving of His life voluntarily for the sins of humankind. As God's prophet, He told His followers about the future of the Kingdom and revealed new truths to them after His death and resurrection.

Jesus' work as a priest will be treated more fully later in this study. His priestly work is that of offering up sacrifice and mediating between God and persons.

As a king, Jesus is ruler over all. In His first coming He founded His Kingdom and claimed authority as the Messiah. He called for perfect obedience, spoke with authority, worked miracles, called forth His church, established the ordinances, died on a cross, conquered the grave, ascended to the right hand of God, and will reign until all His enemies are subdued. He now commissions His followers to preach the gospel to the world, intercedes for His people, sends His presence to fill the church with power, and will come again to receive His people, who will live and reign with Him forever and ever.

Jesus: Divine and Human

Jesus' identity with God was discussed in chapter 2. Jesus is God, and He is man; He is God-man. As God, He perfectly represents God to us; as man, He perfectly represents us to God. Jesus said to His disciples, "'Anyone who has seen me has seen the Father'" (John 14:9), and He claimed, "'I and the Father are one'" (John 10:30). Other texts indicate that Jesus saw Himself in a unique Son relationship to the Father: Matthew 11:25-27; Mark 12:35-37; 13:32; and 14:61-64. Other New Testament texts, too numerous to list, indicate the wide range of His power and authority over nature, demons, the Scriptures, and the forgiveness of sins. But accepting Christ as divine, as God Himself, is a matter of faith. The Bible represents evidence of Jesus' claims, His miraculous power, and His death and resurrection. In the end, however, we come to that certainty by faith, by experiencing Christ in direct encounter, and by knowing that we indeed have met God.

Jesus was divine, and He also was human; but we should use present tense: He *is* divine, and He *is* human. He continues eternally, as such, for He has not lost the humanness that is so essential a part of His understanding of our humanness (see Heb. 4:14-16). Perhaps no text so clearly describes Jesus' humanity as the wilderness temptation experience in Matthew 4:1-11 (see also Mark 1:12-13; Luke 4:1-13).

The experience came just after Jesus' baptism. He was led into the wilderness. The word *led* means *driven;* Jesus was as much under the leadership of God in this experience as when He was baptized. This experience was so crucial in the life and ministry of Jesus that He must have told it to the disciples Himself, for no one else was there with Him.

The purpose of the experience is explicitly stated: "to be tempted by the devil" (Matt. 4:1). The word translated *tempted* is a form of the Greek word *peirazo*. It sometimes is used in the sense of to try, prove, put to the test, or find out what kind of person someone is. Sometimes it is used in the negative sense of trying to trap someone, as the Pharisees attempted with Jesus on several occasions. Sometimes the word is used in the sense of enticement to sin. In fact, the name of Satan in verse 3 is a form of this word. The text, then, can be approached in two ways: (1) Jesus was tested, or (2) Jesus was enticed with the possibility of His sinning.

This difficult text has been approached both ways throughout Christian history. The first approach avoids some difficult problems; for one thing, it keeps us from dealing with Jesus' humanity and the brain-teasing question as to whether Jesus was capable of sinning. On one hand, Hebrews 4:15 asserts that Jesus was tempted in every way just as we are, yet without sin. On the other hand, James 1:13 says, "When tempted, no one should say, 'God is tempting me.' For God cannot be tempted by evil, nor does he tempt anyone."

Part of the answer is that God did not tempt Jesus; Satan did the tempting. Even so, Jesus was led "by the Spirit" into the wilderness for the express purpose of being tempted. A form of the same word is used in the Model Prayer (*peirasmon,* Matt. 6:13), in which we are instructed to pray for God not to lead us into temptation. The idea of this use of the word is that God wants us to grow, and to do so we must at times pass through periods of crucial decision making, times when we set our course or make a great leap of faith to a new level of understanding or commitment. Those are difficult times and fraught with danger, for always at such times we have alternatives that will take us the wrong way. We should dread such times of testing and pray to be delivered from them, but if some alternatives were not wrong and sinful, the decision would not be very important.

Had Jesus yielded to the first temptation, His humanity would have been compromised. In His baptism, Jesus identified with humanity; here Satan attempted to reverse that decision.

Very early in Christian history some heretical ideas developed about the person and work of Christ. These ideas, which would later be known as gnosticism, denied the reality of the incarnation. These false teachers rejected the humanity of Christ because they could not accept the idea that God would have contact with the material, the embodiment of all evil. This heresy taught that the Christ had taken on only the temporary appearance of a man. Adherents did not believe that Jesus Christ had really come in the flesh. Many scholars believe that New Testament writings, especially those of John, oppose these heresies.

Throughout Christian history, scholars have grappled with how Jesus could be 100 percent divine and 100 percent human at the same time. The fact is that the concept does not make sense in human terms. That reality is part of the mystery of Jesus. The

Bible presents Jesus as both fully divine and fully human, and our ways of explaining the biblical material are simply human attempts to grasp the unexplainable.

In some way, Jesus emptied Himself when He came to earth (see Phil. 2:6-8). He did not empty Himself of His divinity, but rather He emptied Himself as divine into a servanthood ministry. Whatever Jesus did in His self-emptying, it resulted in the fact that He truly suffered and died; He truly grew hungry and tired; and He truly was tempted.

Jesus: the Promised Messiah

Messiah means *Anointed One*. Early in Israel's history the anointed one was the human leader, such as David, whom God chose. As time went on, God used the concept to reveal that one day an ideal leader would come and deliver Israel from its oppressors. God began to speak through the prophets about the Anointed One—the Messiah—to come. The prophets used two basic ideas when they proclaimed this coming Messiah. First, He was to be a great King who would lead Israel to become the world's ruling nation. Second, He was to be a Suffering Servant.

The Jews understood and accepted the first group of prophecies, but not the second. During the interbiblical period (the time between the Old and New Testaments), writers of the Apocrypha developed this idea of a political Messiah much more fully, and well before the first century the Jews had accepted the political, military Messiah concept. The Suffering Servant passages were interpreted to apply to Israel as a nation.

The expectation of the Messiah's coming was heavy in the air in Jesus' day. People looked fervently for His coming. When Jesus came and applied the Suffering Servant passages to Himself, they took on new meaning. These passages described a Messiah different from the one expected by the Jews. The religious leaders of Jesus' day resisted the Jews' effort to define the nature of His messiahship.

Jesus' temptation experience not only informs us about His humanity; it also tells us much about His messiahship. Jesus was led by God into the wilderness at this crucial point at the beginning of His ministry for the express purpose of affirming the type of Messiah He would be. He committed Himself irrevocably to be a Suffering Servant Messiah.

Jesus was tempted to change the stone into bread (see Matt. 4:3-4). If He used His power selfishly to meet His own needs, He would be bound to focus His ministry on meeting the selfish needs of others. Yielding to this temptation would force Him to become a bread Messiah, making physical needs the basic thrust of His ministry. Such a messiahship would inspire only shallow commitment and invite the wrong kind of motives in His followers. History already had proved the bread approach wrong, for God performed amazing wonders to free the Hebrews from slavery, and He fed them miraculously in the wilderness; yet they were unfaithful to God as soon as the miracles dimmed slightly in their memory. What God gave was not enough. They wanted leeks and onions and melons. That is the nature of a kingdom built on selfish needs; Jesus did not seek that kind of kingdom.

In the second temptation (see Matt. 4:5-7) Satan took Jesus to a pinnacle of the Temple. The place has been identified by some writers as the southeast corner of the mount overlooking the Kidron Valley, but more likely it was a pinnacle of the Temple proper overlooking the Temple court. Some expected that when the Messiah appeared, He would announce Himself with a miracle in the Temple court. What better way to begin His ministry than for Jesus to take advantage of that expectation and leap from a high point, in full view of the crowds below, in the very court of God's Temple, and to have the people see angels catch Him before His body crushed on the hard stone?

Jesus' first year of ministry could have been called the year of obscurity. Not much detail is given in the Gospels about that year. It was spent primarily in Judea rather than Galilee, where He concentrated during the last two years. Why should Jesus spend a year of obscurity when He could launch His ministry with a spectacular showing and announcement? People would know immediately that He claimed to be the Messiah, and they would have flocked to hear Him speak. Or would they? Would they not rather have flocked to see Him perform yet more miracles? Again, Jesus saw the full implications of the temptation. He would have established Himself as a spectacular Messiah, and

His message would have been ignored and lost in the glamour of miracle working.

The third temptation was a call to Jesus to fall down and worship Satan (see Matt. 4:8-9). How brazen! Satan attacked Jesus at the very point of Jesus' reason for coming to earth: to have all people acknowledge Him as king. Jesus came to save the world; Satan promised that He could have it on a silver platter. How do you suppose Satan could have done that? The *coup* would have been marvelous indeed, for God no longer would be God. Satan would be God, in effect, for Jesus was God incarnate, and Satan would have become His master.

Alexander the Great lived three centuries before Christ. His father, king of Macedon, had begun the conquest of the Greek city-states. Within thirteen years Alexander had conquered the world from Greece to the borders of India. Satan could have done that for Jesus. Many scholars see in this temptation Satan's challenge for Jesus to become a military Messiah. In so doing, Jesus would fulfill the expectations of the Jews of His day. Later, just after Peter had confessed Jesus as the Son of the living God, Peter insisted that Jesus would not be killed as He predicted He would (see Matt. 16:21-23). Jesus' response appears harsh until we realize that Peter, who still believed at that point that Jesus would be a military Messiah, was repeating the third temptation. Jesus already had dealt with that style of messiahship. After Jesus fed the five thousand, the people tried to crown Him king (see John 6:14-15). They would have accepted a military Messiah, especially one who could miraculously feed them anytime they were hungry. To be a military Messiah would have denied all Jesus taught throughout His ministry about servanthood.

Jesus asked His disciples, "'Who do you say I am?'" (Matt. 16:15). Peter spoke for the group: "'You are the Christ, the Son of the living God'" (Matt. 16:16). *Christ* is the Greek word for the Hebrew *Messiah*. The answer was beyond human comprehension; it had come by revelation from God. Jesus then charged His disciples to tell no one that He was the Messiah (see Matt. 16:20). He was not keeping His message silent; He was trying to prevent people from believing the wrong things about His messiahship. The people believed in a political, military Messiah. For that reason, Jesus rarely used the word. He preferred the term *Son of man*, a messianic word from Daniel that He could fill with the meaning He wanted it to have. Jesus' messiahship surprised everyone. He was a redeeming Messiah, one who broke down barriers of race, culture, sex, status, and language to be a Savior for all people everywhere.

Jesus: the High Priest

To come directly into the presence of God was a new idea to the Jews. The holy of holies was a place only the high priest could enter, and he went there only once a year, on the Day of Atonement, after he offered a sacrifice for his sins and those of the people. The sacrifice removed the sin barrier between God and His people.

The writer of Hebrews proclaimed that the barrier no longer is there. Hebrews 10:19-22 describes the new and living way that people can approach God. In times past, a sinful man representing sinful people would bring a sacrifice of a lamb and put it on the altar of God in the presence of God. But sin was always present. Never had a perfect priest existed who could bring a perfect sin offering; but Jesus is the Great High Priest, one who is without sin, one who is perfect in every way. Therefore, the barriers no longer exist. Due to the sacrifice of Jesus and His priestly ministry, every man, woman, and child on earth can come directly into the presence of God. There is no longer a physical holy of holies, no Day of Atonement, no blood sacrifices. None of that is required any longer because of Jesus, our perfect Sacrifice and perfect High Priest. Now we can come directly into the presence of God.

Jesus Christ is the bridge over whom we come into the presence of God Himself and have perfect forgiveness, perfect cleansing, and perfect salvation. Believers await the coming again of a perfect Savior to take us to a perfect heaven that He has prepared for us. Hebrews 7:1-17 speaks of the priesthood of Melchizedek. He was a king and priest of Jerusalem in Abraham's time. There is no record of his genealogy or of his death; he appeared long before the Hebrew priesthood was established; and Abraham offered sacrifices and paid tithes through him. Hebrews uses that example to emphasize some facts about Jesus' priesthood. Although Melchizedek has no genealogical record, Jesus is forever. No record of Melchizedek's death exists, and Jesus rose from the grave and lives forever. Melchizedek appeared before the Old Testament priesthood, and Jesus' priesthood is older and superior. Jesus is not a priest after the Levitical order—an order established in history and begun with humans—but is a priest after the order of Melchizedek, without beginning or end and with a prior claim to God's blessing.

Jesus Himself is the guarantee that the New Testament, the new will God wrote for His people, is better than the old (see Heb. 7:22). We are reminded that human priests die, but Jesus lives forever (see Heb. 7:23-24). Jesus now is on the right hand of God (see Heb. 1:3). His role there, as Hebrews tells us throughout, is not as judge but as mediator. His activity as mediator is not reserved just for the judgment at the end of time. He intercedes to the Father for those who believe in Him. Those who are saved by the shedding of His blood come under His care. Hebrews 4:14-16 encapsulates the whole book of Hebrews. The writer is saying, "Turn your eyes upon Jesus." What is the faith we are to hold to so tenaciously? This passage lists five elements. The first one is that we have a Great High Priest. *Great* is *megan*, as in *megalopolis*, a great, expansive string of cities. There is no great greater than *megan*. "Gone through" (v. 14) refers to a completed action; Jesus has done His work and is one with God, where He shall be forever. The Greek word in verse 15 that is translated *sympathize* refers to experience rather than just intellectual knowledge. We have a High Priest who has experienced everything we feel.

John Foster, a diplomat for Britain during World War II, had to flee China when the Japanese approached. One day he came home and looked in on his teenage daughter. She was leaning over the radio and listening to a news broadcast announcing that Japanese tanks had rolled into Canton. The daughter began to weep slowly, then broke into loud sobs, her body shaking with despair. Foster recalled that many people heard that broadcast, but few were touched by it as she was. Why? Because she had been born there, had lived there, and had gone to school there.

Her nurses, teachers, and friends were there. She knew the streets and the shops. She understood more than others because she had been there.[1] Hebrews tells us that Jesus has been there. He understands our heartaches, our pains, and our way of life.

Jesus: Lord and King

"Jesus is Lord" is the earliest Christian creedal statement in the New Testament. Paul reminded the Corinthians that the primary test of fellowship was the lordship of Christ (1 Cor. 12:3). The title *Lord* is used throughout the New Testament. Christ assumed the title *Lord* for Himself in Matthew 7:21-22; 22:41-45. When Thomas saw the scars in the hands of the resurrected Jesus, he cried out, "'My Lord and my God'" (John 20:28).

The next great awakening could well develop around a doctrinal study of Christ's lordship. The Great Awakening of the eighteenth century developed around several of the great neglected doctrines of the faith. The next great revival under Charles Finney centered on the urgent necessity of immediate repentance and acceptance of the pardon offered at the cross. The next major revival centered on prayer and God's power to respond to man's plea. Dwight L. Moody was used as the leader of the next great revival, which focused on the concept of God's love for sinners. Each of these revival movements has focused on some previously neglected Christian doctrine. The lordship of Christ has been neglected in this generation. Studying this doctrine will give us an opportunity to allow the Holy Spirit to speak to us through His Word, and out of this study the Lord may choose to bring revival to our world.

The New Testament often asserts Jesus' lordship. He is called the "only Ruler, the King of kings, and Lord of lords" (1 Tim. 6:15); He is "the ruler of the kings of the earth" (Rev. 1:5). Pilate asked Jesus, "'Are you the king of the Jews?'" (John 18:33). Jesus answered, "'My kingdom is not of this world'" (John 18:36). Pilate then said, "'You are a king, then!'" (John 18:37). Jesus answered, "'You are right in saying I am a king.'"

Hebrews 1:2 tells us that God has appointed Jesus "heir of all things." God has put everything in the universe in the hands of Jesus (see Ps. 2:8; Eph. 1:10). The early church believed that

Jesus was heir of the Kingdom and all the universe. That was part of the message they proclaimed.

Christ is Lord of all the angels (Heb. 1:4-6). The Jews thought a great deal about angels and attributed to them great power and prestige. But the writer of Hebrews reminded them that the angels are but the servants of Jesus. They are sent out by Him to do God's work in this world.

Hebrews 1:3 shows Jesus with the Kingdom scepter in His hand. But what is the nature of this Kingdom? After Jesus' resurrection the disciples asked, "'Lord, are you at this time going to restore the kingdom to Israel?'" (Acts 1:6). Jesus' answer to their question must not be underestimated. Jesus told His disciples quite clearly that their task was not "to know the times or dates the Father has set by his own authority" (Acts 1:7). They had to cut themselves loose from the political-power concept of the Kingdom. The point for the disciples was that they would receive the power of the Holy Spirit and become witnesses throughout the world, at home and abroad, to all peoples in all places.

Speaking of Jesus' ascension into heaven, Luke wrote "while he was blessing them, he left them and was taken up into heaven" (Luke 24:51). After the blessing, they watched Him ascend (see Acts 1:9). It was important that the disciples saw Jesus physically in that act. They knew and we know, for all time, exactly where Jesus went. Heaven is His home, and it will be ours. The Kingdom was to do with heavenly things, not with earthly power and wealth. The center of God's Kingdom was not to be Jerusalem the earthly, but Jerusalem the heavenly. Ascending to be with His Father emphasized to the disciples throughout history that Jesus is one with the Father, that His claim to be King of kings and Lord of lords of all the universe is true, that His work of redemption was completed, and that the one who had emptied Himself was returning to His glory.

When Jesus was received into that cloud, He was received to be enthroned, to reign. Once again He took His place on the right hand of His Father. That is where His place is. From that time until now and into the future, the enthroned Christ is preparing this world to present it to the Father. We ought to break into the "Hallelujah Chorus"! He is and will be King of kings and Lord of lords. What He now is will be made complete at the end of the age, and what we are working with Him to accomplish will be accomplished through His power and wisdom (1 Cor. 15:24-26).

Christ's work in this world is moving toward that great time when "at the name of Jesus every knee should bow, in heaven and on earth and under the earth, and every tongue confess that Jesus Christ is Lord, to the glory of God the Father" (Phil. 2:10–11). He is "sustaining all things by His powerful word" (Heb. 1:3). He is the alpha and omega, the A to Z, the first, the last, and all in between. Never has there been or will be a moment when God has left this world to itself. Jesus always has been involved in making this universe work (see Col. 1:16–17). The reference to thrones, powers, rulers, and authorities indicates Jesus' continuing activity in the affairs of this world. All Jesus has to do is speak, and things happen. He spoke, and demons were exorcised; people were healed and forgiven; and the fig tree withered. That same power moves people and nations today.

PERSONAL LEARNING ACTIVITY 4

Read Hebrews 4:14-16.
1. According to verse 14, who is our Great High Priest?

_____

2. What do you believe is meant by verse 15, which tells us that Jesus was "tempted in every way, just as we are"?

_____

_____

_____

_____

_____

3. How does Jesus give us confidence when we need mercy and grace?

_____

_____

_____

_____

_____

1. *The Letter to the Hebrews*, The Daily Study Bible Series, rev. ed., trans. by William Barclay (Philadelphia: The Westminster Press, 1976), 43-44.

CHAPTER 5

The Atoning Work of Christ

*Now he has appeared once for all at the end of the
ages to do away with sin by the sacrifice of himself.*
Hebrews 9:26

Rom. 5:11 (KJV)

"I owed a debt I could not pay;
HE paid a debt HE did not owe."

DEBT = SIN

THE ATONEMENT IS A SUBJECT IN
which Christians have always been vitally in-
terested. The word itself has been popularly explained by break-
ing the word down: at-one-ment, bringing the person who is
estranged from God into a reconciled relationship with God. But
exactly how did Jesus' death on the cross accomplish this? Many
scholars throughout history have explained the atonement in
various ways. None of the theories exhaust or fully explain it.

On this point all traditional scholars agree: The cross is at the
very center of the Christian message. Whatever Christ did on the
cross was completely adequate for human sin. God's love lay behind it. He planned the action, initiated it, completed it, and
honors it. God loved humankind beyond comprehension. The
pain of our separation from Him was real to God, and He took
action to solve the sin problem. Any theory of the atonement that
does not take into account the love of God is faulty. Love was the
dominating force behind the atonement.

Before the beginning of time God decided how He wanted to
reach out and touch the hearts of humans with His love. Before
the foundation of the world God planned Jesus' coming to earth
(see 1 Pet. 1:20). Before the foundation of the world God planned
for believers to be saved by Jesus' coming (see Eph. 1:4).
Sin prevented people from being reconciled to God. That

65

problem had to be solved. Sin is repulsive to a holy God; sin must be judged; the sin barrier had to be removed. In seeking to explain the atonement, some pit God's wrath and justice against His love and mercy so that God seems to have two natures at war with each other. That view is useful in emphasizing that God's justice requires satisfaction and that God's mercy will redeem. It is not accurate if God is pitted against Himself. A human parent loves a wayward child even when the child has to be corrected. The parent is not therefore dealing with two natures at war with each other; the parent is a whole person who seeks the best for the child even when the child does wrong. God is a whole Person, too. He never stops loving us even when we are sinful. It was God's love that found a way to solve the sin problem in a manner that is both loving and just.

The work of Christ is expressed in a number of words, none of which is adequate in itself. Christ's atonement and the resultant change in a person's life are so many-faceted that they must be viewed from a variety of angles. As with a prism turned slowly in the hand, a different color is revealed as a different ray strikes it. Some of the words are long ones, but they are well worth learning for the powerful truths they convey.

Christs' Atonement: Substitution

Christ was crucified as a substitute for us. The word *substitute* is not found in Scripture in connection with the atonement, but several texts teach the truth of substitution. Romans 3:24-26 has three key atonement words: *justified, redemption, and sacrifice.* The thrust of the text is that Christ died in our place. The idea of ransom (see Mark 10:45) is that since Christ died, we do not. Paul wrote that Jesus was made to be sin for us (see 2 Cor. 5:21) and was made a curse for us (see Gal. 3:13). Although some modern people have trouble accepting the idea that one Person can legitimately pay another person's penalty, the New Testament is clear, in these and other texts, that Jesus' death was a substitute for ours. If it was not, then the sin problem has not been solved.

Christ's Atonement: Covenant

The concept of covenant is not familiar to many Christians.

When we speak of covenant, we generally think in terms of believers covenanting together as a church. We make certain commitments to one another and to Christ. This use of the word is valid, but a great deal more lies behind the biblical meaning of covenant. An understanding of the concept is central to understanding Jesus' atonement.

We must distinguish between covenant and promise. The Bible is full of promises but records only a few covenants. The first covenant is the one God made with Noah. A major and crucial part of that covenant was that it was made for the benefit of all people, not just one nation (see Gen. 9:9-10,12,15-17). Thus, this covenant reveals to us that God's plan of history includes all people. The covenants that followed were intended by God as ways to reach all humankind.

The second covenant we will consider is God's covenant with Abraham. God specified His purpose for this covenant that "all peoples on earth will be blessed through you" (Gen. 12:3). Abraham was to father a nation whom God would train and use in order to reach out to all humankind. A continual theme of the Old Testament is Israel's failure to understand the purpose of its calling.

The third covenant was the Sinai covenant. In it, God shaped the Hebrews into a nation and gave them a charter to be a showcase nation to the whole world. Had Israel kept God's covenant— observed His laws and purpose—they would have demonstrated to all the world what life would be if people lived as God intended. The people of Israel did not fulfill their part of the Sinai covenant. They demanded that Samuel, God's appointed leader, anoint a king to rule over them (see 1 Sam. 8:4-5). Samuel did not want to do this because he recognized it as a rejection of God's kingship over His people. God told Samuel pointedly, "'It is not you they have rejected as their king, but me'" (1 Sam. 8:7). Soon thereafter, Samuel anointed Saul to be Israel's first king.

When David succeeded Saul as king of Israel, God promised that a descendent of David would rule over God's people forever (see 2 Sam. 7:11-16). This promise found fulfillment in the coming of Jesus, the Messiah (see Luke 1:32-33).

Because the Sinai covenant and the Davidic covenant were ir-reconcilable, they account for much of the conflict between the kings and the prophets throughout the Old Testament. The Sinai covenant allowed for no king but God. The Davidic covenant promised a king from David's line forever. Only in Jesus Christ could the opposing covenants be reconciled, for He is divine (thus, no king rules between God and His people), and He is a descendant of David (who, as King of kings, rules forever over God's people).

The problem with the Old Testament covenants was that they did not provide the inner power necessary to keep them. The law was helpful but inadequate. Jeremiah prophesied that the day would come when God's law would be written on the heart (see Jer. 31:33-34). That prophecy was fulfilled in the new covenant made possible by Jesus' atoning death. He died, reconciling all who would believe. The new covenant is one of inner power, based not on law but on a free, redeemed relationship with God through Christ.

Christ's Atonement: Sacrifice

Recently I read an extensive article on India. As I read it, I noticed particularly the many worship and sacrificial processes in that great country. Many gods and goddesses are worshiped. The marriages of the deities are celebrated. The holy Ganges River is believed to bring healing if one can get into it at the right time.

As in India, people all over the world are looking for some-thing that will save them from their sins, something that will bring hope and peace to their lives. Forgiveness and peace are available through the gospel of Jesus Christ. Hebrews 7:25 says, "Therefore he is able to save completely those who come to God through him, because he always lives to intercede for them." Jesus did not die to condemn people but to save them completely, regardless of who they are, what they have done, or what they believe. The word *completely* in this verse does not refer to time but to a state of completion. Jesus wants to save, completely, everyone on earth.

The priestly work of Jesus was accomplished in His atoning death. He who knew no sin became the sin bearer for humankind. Through union with Him, men and women enter a new life and will in the end share the sinlessness of Christ. In the death of Christ on the cross, the God of holy love overcame sin through His own sacrifice.

At first, the disciples looked on the death of Jesus as a cruel defeat. They were dejected and despondent until Jesus rose from the grave. When the disciples opened their hearts to the teachings of the resurrected Jesus, they realized what He had done for them (see Luke 24:45-47).

The full importance of this work of Jesus can be understood only as we study sacrifice in the Old Testament. Limited space allows only the mention of the four types of sacrifice that are prominent in New Testament references: the burnt, peace, sin, and guilt offerings. Leon Morris lists six steps common to sacrifice: (1) the drawing near in worship; (2) the laying on of hands, which symbolized the transference of personal sins onto the sacrifice; (3) the killing of the animal by the worshiper (not the priest), which indicated that the worshiper was worthy of death; (4) the various ways the blood was applied in rituals, which began the priest's work and which indicated the seriousness of sin; (5) the burning of the sacrifice on the altar, with the smoke and aroma ascending to God, thus offering the sacrifice to God; and (6) the disposal of the carcass, in which various parts of the remainder of the sacrifice were distributed in a variety of ways, each of which had its significance involving the people in the ritual.[2]

All of these steps are part of the understanding of the first-century Jew—and indeed of the Gentile, too, for he also had sacrifices—and make up the background of Jesus' sacrifice. The difference was that Jesus' sacrifice was perfect and does not have to be repeated. He was our sacrifice, and no longer are sacrifices necessary.

Hebrews 7:26-27, referring to the priesthood of Jesus, says: "Such a high priest meets our need—one who is holy, blameless, pure, set apart from sinners, exalted above the heavens. Unlike the other high priests, he does not need to offer sacrifices day after day, first for his own sins, and then for the sins of the people. He sacrificed for their sins once for all when he offered himself." He is holy; no other attempt at purification is needed. He is blameless (Greek *akakos*, entirely innocent), pure (Greek *amiantos*, undefiled), and set apart from sinners. No more perfect sacrifice will exist. He is exalted above the heavens; no greater sacrifice will ever be needed. His perfect sacrifice and perfect priesthood are forever sufficient. All of these qualifications stand in contrast to earthly high priests, who changed with each generation. These high priests could not save. They were mortal and sinful, like all other humans. Their sacrifices were imperfect and temporary. They were human mediators with human limitations. Jesus is able to save completely those who come to Him (see Heb. 7:25). This means no sinner is so bad that he cannot be saved.

2 COR. 5:21
1 PETER 2:24

Christs Atonement: Redemption

Jesus' death redeemed us from sin. This means liberation and freedom for the believer (see Gal. 5:1). In the ancient world slavery was commonplace. A person could be born a slave, be made a slave as a prisoner of war, or be kidnapped by slave traders. Once a person was a slave, his children also were slaves, unless a person or a group paid a ransom and redeemed them. In the spiritual realm God paid that ransom with His blood, and it was entirely sufficient. Scholars in Christian history have speculated as to whom Jesus paid the ransom, sometimes going to considerable lengths to describe the transaction. Such speculation tends to create more problems than it solves. The primary New Testament point is that Christ set us free, the emphasis being on the incredible power of God to accomplish in Christ that which nothing else before had been able to accomplish. Freedom is full and complete in Jesus Christ.

The Person of Jesus and the redemptive work of Jesus go together. Paul said, "'Believe in the Lord Jesus, and you will be saved'" (Acts 16:31). Jesus did not come to earth on a mission of teaching and preaching alone. He came to do something that could not be accomplished without Calvary. He said, "'The Son of Man came to seek and to save what was lost'" (Luke 19:10). Peter declared of Christ at Pentecost, "'This man was handed over to you by God's set purpose and foreknowledge; and you, with the help of wicked men, put him to death by nailing him to the cross'" (Acts 2:23). Paul said, "God made him who had no sin to be sin for us, so that in him we might become the righteousness of God" (2 Cor. 5:21). Redemption is the result of the willingness of God's Son to bear our sins in His body so that we *NOTE* might die to sin and live to righteousness (see 1 Pet. 2:24).

Why would God allow the cross? The best explanation is given by Jesus: "'Just as Moses lifted up the snake in the desert, so the Son of Man must be lifted up, that everyone who believes in him may have eternal life'" (John 3:14-15). In the cross God has done for sinners what they could not do for themselves.

Jesus redeemed us from all iniquity. All of our sins are under His blood.

Christ's Atonement: Reconciliation   *Titus 3:5-7*

T. W. Hunt tells in *The Doctrine of Prayer* of counseling a woman and finally reaching her with the question "If Jesus' blood cleans you, how clean can you be?"[1] I was training counselors in Dayton, Ohio, for an evangelistic crusade. A counselor brought to the crusade a young woman whom she had won to Christ. The woman was a drug addict, and her arms had many needle marks. She was also a prostitute, put on the street by her mother at age ten to support her mother's drug habit. When she came forward at the crusade to make her decision public, she said: "I've met Jesus today, and He made me clean. I'm no longer dirty and filthy. I'm clean again."

Christ died to reconcile estranged people to God. The word *reconciliation* pictures a separation, an enmity between each person and God because of sin (see Rom. 5:10). Christ brought God and persons who believe on Him into a right relationship. God is not the one who changes; reconciliation is not the process of changing God so that He will smile on us. Sin separates us from God. The sin problem had to be dealt with, for God stands in opposition to sin and evil. But God initiated a way to reconciliation (see Rom. 5:11). It is we who are changed, we who are reconciled to God, not God to us (see 2 Cor. 5:18-20; Col. 1:21-22).

Reconciliation does not mean *reformation* or *"getting religion."* Nor does it mean that estranged equals are brought back together. The sovereign God, who could justly judge us, has acted to provide a way to transform us through a new birth (see John 3). *Born again* is a combination of two words. The first Greek word, *gennethe*, is translated *is born*. The second Greek word, *anothen*, has three meanings: *from above; from the beginning;* and *again, anew*. The idea of rebirth and recreation is found in many New Testament Scriptures (see Rom. 6:11; Gal. 6:15; Titus 3:5; Jas. 1:18; 1 Pet. 1:3,23; 1 John 2:29; 3:9; 4:7; 5:1,4,18).

God did not create us to be estranged from Him. When we are reconciled, we begin the process of becoming what we were created to be: persons at peace with God and with one another (see Eph. 2:11-21). Our world is filled with much strife, hostility, and war. Christ is the way to peace. When people are truly reconciled in Christ and when they seek to follow His teachings, true peace results.

Christ's Atonement: Propitiation/Expiation (Rom. 3:21-26)

Theologians differ in their interpretations of the biblical teachings on propitiation/expiation. Both of these words are used to translate the Greek word *hilasmos*. In various forms this word appears in Romans 3:25; Hebrews 2:17; 1 John 2:2; 4:10. The King James Version translates this word as *propitiation* (except in Heb. 2:17, where it is translated "to make reconciliation"). The Revised Standard Version translates *hilasmos* and other forms of the word as *expiation*. The difference is significant. According to the *Dictionary of the Bible*, edited by James Hastings and revised by Frederick C. Grant and H. H. Rowley, *propitiation* refers to appeasing an angry or offended person, while *expiation* has to do with removing sin or guilt.

Those who prefer to translate *hilasmos* as *expiation* emphasize that the sinner is reconciled to God through the sacrifice of Christ. God provides the means for this reconciliation by removing the cause of our alienation from God. Sin is expiated by the sacrifice of Christ. Thus, that which separates us from God is removed, and our approach to God is made possible through Christ. *Expiation* does not focus on appeasing the wrath of God but on the action of God, through Christ, to remove the barrier of sin that separates sinners from God.

Other scholars, such as Leon Morris, prefer to translate

hilasmos and other forms of the word as *propitiation*. These theologians feel that the idea of expiation neglects what the Bible teaches about the wrath of God against sin.[2] Millard J. Erickson writes, "The numerous passages that speak of the wrath of God against sin are evidence that Christ's death was necessarily propitiatory."[3] Referring to various passages on the atonement in the writings of Paul, Erickson writes, "So then, Paul's idea of the atoning death . . . is not simply that it covers sin and cleanses from its corruption (expiation), but that the sacrifice also appeases a God who hates sin and is radically opposed to it (propitiation)."[4]

Note 1

The *New International Version* uses neither *propitiation* nor *expiation* to translate *hilasmos*. Rather, in 1 John 2:2; 4:10 the word is translated "atoning sacrifice." In a similar way, the *New International Version* translates *hilasterion* in Romans 3:25 as "a sacrifice of atonement" and *hilaskesthai* in Hebrews 2:17 as "make atonement." Whichever view one holds in this matter, the crucial truth is that the problem of human sin and separation from God was addressed and answered in the sacrifice of Jesus on the cross.

Christ's Atonement: Justification   *Rom. 5:12-21*

Justification is one of the most prominent concepts in the New Testament. The Greek word, usually translated *justice* or *righteousness* in various nouns, verbs, or other forms, occurs many times. The two ways of translating the word indicate rightly that the two concepts are not separate ones in the Bible. Justice must be righteous. It must rest on an ethical base of holiness. Righteousness must result in justice. Thus, God's demand for righteousness through the Old Testament prophets is fulfilled only when justice prevails throughout the land. The connection is just as sure in the New Testament. A just God justifies us; a righteous God makes us righteous.

The Old Testament concept of justice and righteousness was based on keeping the law. The New Testament concept is based on Jesus Christ. We who believe in Jesus as Savior and Lord have Christ's righteousness imputed to us. Justice is served completely in what Christ did for us in redemption (see Rom. 3:25). The idea must have been current in Paul's day that God must not be just if He forgives sin so easily. Paul argued that God's justice is fulfilled in His providing a way for sinful people to be made righteous, in Christ (see Rom. 3:26). We come to Christ through faith alone, not by works; Christ as righteousness for us is a gift from God to those who believe (see Rom. 5:17). Those who seek to secure their salvation through works are reverting to the concept of salvation by works (see Rom. 9:30-32).

Justification may appear too easy to modern people, but it certainly was not easy for God. Leon Morris illustrated the difficulty this way: A tramp breaks into your house and steals something expensive and precious, but you forgive him in the end. This forgiveness may be difficult, but not as difficult as if you discovered that the thief was your best friend. Now you feel betrayed, and forgiveness comes much harder. But suppose you find that the thief is your son. All kinds of emotions well up in you. You will forgive him, for that is the nature of parenthood, but you certainly will not find the forgiving to be easy.[5] God forgives all those who will come to Christ in faith. His forgiveness is not easy; yet He not only forgives but also justifies us, makes us just as though we had not sinned. The fact of justification is a miracle of God that is beyond full comprehension.

Ralph Neighbour has said, "Jesus can never look at me without seeing His own blood. Because I asked Him to forgive me and cleanse me with His blood, no one in heaven can look at me without seeing me through the blood of Jesus Christ."

PERSONAL LEARNING ACTIVITY 5

In chapter 5 the author uses several words to describe the atonement. Briefly define each word on the lines below.

1. Substitution: _____

_____

2. Covenant: _____

_____

3. Sacrifice: _____

_____

4. Redemption: _____

_____

5. Reconciliation: _____

_____

6. Expiation: _____

_____

7. Justification: _____

_____

8. Propitiation: _____

_____

_____

1. T. W. Hunt, *The Doctrine of Prayer* (Nashville: Convention Press, 1986), 62.
2. Leon Morris, *The Atonement* (Downers Grove: InterVarsity Press, 1983), 45-50. Used by permission.
3. Millard J. Erickson, *Christian Theology* (Grand Rapids: Baker Book House, 1985), 811.
4. Ibid.
5. Morris, 200.

CHAPTER 6

The Doctrine of Salvation

"God so loved the world that he gave his one and
only Son, that whoever believes in him shall not
perish but have eternal life."
John 3:16

S IN IS A REALITY IN HUMAN LIFE. The results of human sin can be seen everywhere, and individual lives are often deeply scarred by sin.

David expressed the deep need of all people when he called on God to make him clean from sin (see Ps. 51:7). Isaiah held out hope for sinful people when he said, "'Though your sins are like scarlet, they shall be as white as snow; though they are red as crimson, they shall be like wool'" (Isa. 1:18). God's saving plan found its fulfillment in Jesus Christ.

The main work of Jesus is to save. That is the meaning of His name, and it is often stated as His work (Luke 19:10; 1 Tim. 1:15; Heb. 9:26). Salvation is wholly the result of God's love. That fact is stated in the best-known Bible verse, John 3:16. That verse tells us that God's love is universal: "'God so loved the world.'" Few passages in the Bible so stress and underline God's universal gospel as does this passage. A preacher once said, "God's will to save is as wide as His will to create." God loves all the multitudes of people in our world today. All races, colors, and nationalities, whether good or bad—God loves them all. God loves the unlovely and the unlovable, the person who worships God and the person who never thinks of God. Augustine said, "God loves each one of us as if there was only one of us to love."

The missionary heart is not an option for the Christian; if we are in tune with God, we are burdened for His world.

GRACE God's love is unmerited, undeserved. God gave His one and only Son. Many people in the history of this world have rejected God. The pages of history are full of murder, killing, dishonesty, wars, and injustice. Many have chosen to resist and reject God. Yet He has loved all people with love that they do not deserve. This gift of salvation is given to all who will believe simply because God is gracious (see Eph. 2:8-10).

Salvation: by Grace Through Faith

Paul makes it very clear that we are saved by the grace of God. *Grace* is one of the most beautiful words in the Bible. It means *favor, thanks, goodwill,* and *gratitude,* carrying the essence of goodness, gentleness, and helpfulness. Basically, the word means *to make a gift.* The Greek word for *grace, charis,* speaks of God's redemptive love, which is always active to save sinners and to maintain them in a proper relationship with Him.

The Bible is the story of God's saving grace. The Old Testament pictures God's loving-kindness through His covenant relationships with people. In the New Testament we find a new covenant in God's gift of Jesus: "The law was given through Moses; grace and truth came through Jesus Christ" (John 1:17).

Salvation does not come as the result of faith in Christ plus our good works. In Galatians 5:4 Paul speaks of those who are "fallen away from grace," but he does not mean that one who is in grace has fallen out of grace. He charged the Galatians with falling away from teaching salvation by grace. Salvation can come only by God's grace.

SALVATION: By GRACE, THROUGH HIS SPIRIT.

Salvation: Steps in the Plan

1. *Conviction.* I heard the gospel for the first time when I was fifteen years of age. I was a lost boy in a lost family in a pagan society. Yet when I heard about Jesus, I never questioned the fact that it was the truth. When I went to a church service because I had nothing else to do and heard the pastor preach and then give the invitation, I walked down the aisle and told the pastor that I was lost, going to hell, and wanted to accept Jesus as my Savior. I

knelt with the pastor and prayed "the sinner's prayer" of confession and acceptance. How can a fifteen-year-old boy who knew nothing about religion, the Bible, or Christ come to such a quick understanding? It is possible because God worked in my heart to reveal the truth about Jesus. I have preached on mission fields to people who never heard of Christ; yet they came to accept Christ as soon as the invitation was given and said: "I have never heard this before, but there is something about it that speaks to me. I believe it and accept Jesus as my Savior." On one occasion I preached to a crowd in Africa while a group of detractors paraded outside, beating drums and calling on their god to curse the meeting. When the invitation was given, thirty-five persons who had never heard of Christ accepted Him as Savior.

The truth that Jesus is the Son of God is so profound that God's revelation is required for it to be understood. Paul wrote, "No one can say, 'Jesus is Lord,' except by the Holy Spirit" (1 Cor. 12:3). Jesus said, "'No one can come to me unless the Father who sent me draws him'" (John 6:44). So when people stand and confess that Jesus is Lord, they do so by divine revelation; God has worked in their hearts to lead them to that understanding.

2. *Repentance.* There are many false and deceptive ideas in the world. Sometimes these erroneous ideas are taught by religious leaders. I recently heard a preacher say that the New Testament teaches no sexual ethic. Of course, this is not true. I once received a letter claiming that no text in the Bible teaches that a hell exists. That, too, is a false idea. Wrong beliefs and wrong behaviors need to be changed. That is what repentance is all about. The New Testament word for *repentance* is *metanoia.* This word expresses three major ideas: a change of mind; a feeling of regret and remorse; and a turning away from sin and to God.

Good

Repentance is the process of admitting the filth and impurity of sin. Isaiah 1:5-6 pictures sin clearly: "Why should you be beaten anymore? Why do you persist in rebellion? Your whole head is injured, your whole heart afflicted. From the sole of your foot to the top of your head there is no soundness—only wounds and welts and open sores, not cleansed or bandaged or soothed with oil."

Repentance recognizes that sin has power and mastery over life (see John 8:34-44). I once heard of some men and women who had taken some defective heroin, and it had paralyzed them, frozen them in one position. That is what sin does; it freezes us in position, taking over and destroying all that it touches. People often try to justify their wrongdoing. They may claim that they are just living their own lives or claiming their right to happiness. As they do this, they often ignore the feelings and well-being of others. More seriously, they ignore the clear teachings of the Bible. But God's Word never changes; His Word tells it like it is. The Bible calls such self-centered living sin. Sin is natural to the person who does not know God or chooses to reject God's truth. Galatians 5:19-21 says: "The acts of the sinful nature are obvious: sexual immorality, impurity and debauchery; idolatry and witchcraft; hatred, discord, jealousy, fits of rage, selfish ambition, dissensions, factions and envy; drunkenness, orgies, and the like. I warn you, as I did before, that those who live like this will not inherit the kingdom of God."

Repentance means three things: *First, it means allowing God to* A- *change your mind*. The only way God can bring cleansing and restore fellowship is for the unsaved person to change radically the way he or she thinks about right and wrong. *Second, it means* B. *allowing God to change your heart*. The emotional basis of life is thoroughly regenerated. Feelings—not just intellectual knowledge—about right and wrong bring the redeemed person to hate sin as God does. *Third, it means allowing God to change your ac-* C. *tions*. Salvation results in a change in conduct. The redeemed person stops doing things that are outside the law of God. But more, the change is positive. The saved person starts living redemptively.

3. *Acceptance*. When a person accepts Christ as Savior, he must accept Him as Lord as well. Salvation is not primarily *from* eternal death but *to* eternal life. The new birth is the beginning of a new life; that is, the life into which the believer is born starts at the moment of conversion. You are not *going* to be born again when you go to heaven; you *are* born again. Life is new and radically different in nature and direction.

No one can be educated into salvation; a decision to accept

His way is the only way!

Christ must be made. You can study a lifetime about Jesus and never know Him as Savior. Teachers of comparative religion all over the world have no trouble placing Jesus among the great leaders and teachers of the world and can quote His words with ease. Some non-Christian religions readily accept Jesus alongside other religious figures. But Jesus is more than a great teacher. Jesus made it clear to Nicodemus that even though he was a moral man and a religious leader, he had to be born again. The Ten Commandments and the Golden Rule are good to live by, but they are not enough to save.

No one is naturally born into the Kingdom. Human birth and spiritual birth are two different things. Every person is born with a nature that is sinful (see Ps. 51:5; Isa. 53:6). There must be spiritual rebirth. Nicodemus was a respectable human being, but Jesus said that he had to be born again. My father had difficulty understanding salvation. He was a good man and was working hard to get better, but he could not find salvation. Once while I was talking with him at 2:00 AM I said: "Dad, you never will become a Christian by working at it as you are. You will never accept Jesus by trying to get your life straight." Suddenly, the spiritual blindness of my Dad was gone, and he began to see the truth of salvation. He prayed, "God, forgive me and save me." Salvation came at the moment of acceptance. When Dad accepted Christ and let Christ do the saving, he was saved.

FAITH makes a good acrostic for the essentials of salvation: Forsaking All, I Trust Him. Jesus made it clear that He is the authority for salvation. Whatever anyone thinks about salvation or wishes it to be is irrelevant. Christ sets the way; He is the authority. For that reason, we must give up our ideas and yield to Christ.

Confession. We sometimes hear of so-called secret believers, people who believe Jesus to be the Son of God, accept Him for personal salvation, but do not openly confess Him because of fear of embarrassment, reprisals, or persecution. Although we are not in a position to judge the sincerity of anyone's faith, Jesus clearly taught the necessity for open confession (see Matt. 10:32-33). Clearly, salvation is not just cognitive assent; it involves commitment to Christ as Lord.

Open confession of Christ speaks to the very nature of faith. Saving faith demands that Christ be first. No one is saved who puts houses or brothers or sisters or father or mother or children or lands before Christ (see Matt. 19:29). Faith is trust and obedience. It is stepping out of neutrality and taking a stand for Christ. It involves making public confession. Can one be saved without being a disciple? How may one receive so marvelous a gift as salvation and yet refuse to be a disciple? How can a true believer not be open about faith in Christ? How can one believe that eternal life is vastly more important than earthly life and yet fail to take a stand for Christ because of fear?

A good case could be argued that the intent of Matthew 10:32-33 is to state the ongoing way that believers should live. A great deal of growth lies ahead for any new believer, and best intentions are subject to the constant pressures of the world. Even Peter denied his Lord. But at the moment of conversion it is inconceivable that the newly saved person would harbor in his heart the intent not to announce his salvation. In Southern Baptist churches the invitation time is designed to provide an immediate opportunity for the new believer to confess to all assembled that he or she has accepted Christ. Baptism usually follows quickly, for it also is a public statement of faith. These are beginnings, not endings, to a life of public confession.

This new beginning deserves the best attention that the church can give. Trained counselors are needed in every church to work with the new converts. At the time of conversion the plan of salvation needs to be made clear. All questions need to be answered, and the new convert needs to leave that initial meeting with printed Scriptures on how to become a Christian and how to have assurance of salvation. The *Personal Commitment Guide* is a good example of this kind of material. Satan is always quick to attack a new Christian with doubts and temptations. We must do all that we can to provide the new Christian with the armor of God and the sword of the Word.

Salvation: the Nature of Saving Faith

The faith required for salvation is more than an optimistic outlook on life. It is also more than giving assent to certain statements of belief. Faith calls for a total response, involving the mind, emotions, and will of the believer.

A. *Saving faith is intellectual.* Saving faith is not blind faith. Facts about God's work with His creation and the life and work of Christ are a matter of record. Some of the facts stretch the human mind. The miracles of Jesus, His virgin birth, His death on the cross, and His resurrection have caused many to reject salvation. Faith chooses to accept the facts that are crucial to salvation.

The question often is asked, What does a person have to know to be saved? This is not an easy question to answer. Salvation comes as a person puts faith in Jesus Christ. Obviously, after a person is saved, he will need to learn many important truths. The more we know about our Christian faith, the better. Three facts, however, are essential to know and accept at the moment of conversion: (1) Jesus really existed as a historical person (see 1 John 1:1-3; 4:2-3); (2) Jesus Christ is the Son of God, and acceptance of Christ on this basis is saving faith (see 1 John 4:15); and (3) Jesus is the way to salvation (see Acts 4:12).

B. *Saving faith is emotional.* People are different; some respond to salvation with great emotion, while others do not. Everyone, however, has emotions. Salvation involves the whole person, and emotions must be part of the experience. Emotion comes as the result of realizing that we have been forgiven of our sins and given a new life. The redemption we experience in Christ brings a powerful change to life. Tears may or may not be shed, but the depth of the salvation experience touches the very depths of the soul. Emotion alone, though, does not result in salvation, no matter how powerful the emotion may be.

C. *Saving faith is volitional.* Volition relates to the will and indicates that salvation is a matter of conscious choosing. The meaning of *faith* has become obscured in the modern world. Sometimes the word is used to refer to believing a set of facts. Sometimes when people speak of a faith, they mean a church or denomination. Sometimes the word is used to refer to a vague mystical feeling. The biblical meaning of faith, however, includes profound commitment. Christ emphasized the need to count the cost of believing and to make an unqualified commitment (see

Luke 14:25-33). Paul is one who counted the cost and chose Christ (see Phil. 3:7-9).

The reality of the human condition, the fact that we still have our sinful nature, is that we never yield ourselves completely to Christ. The growing believer constantly finds rooms and corners of his life that have not been turned over to Christ. Although this is true, at the point of conversion individuals must not consciously withhold any part of themselves; so far as they know themselves, they must choose to turn themselves over completely to Christ.

Salvation: What It Means to Believers

Salvation is an all-encompassing experience. God's saving power reaches to the depth of the being and brings forgiveness, joy, peace, and a new life in Christ. Several important statements describe what salvation means to those who believe.

Salvation is threefold. Salvation includes three dimensions: becoming a believer in Jesus at the point of decision, the continuing life of discipleship, and final redemption. Baptists often have expressed this threefold emphasis this way: I *am* saved, I *am being* saved, and I *will be* saved. The first refers to the need for a decision to be made about Christ. The second refers to the process of Christian growth in which we work out our own salvation (see Phil. 2:12). This does not refer to works salvation; rather, it is the working out in daily life of the salvation experience in the power of the Holy Spirit. The third refers to the time when we meet Christ in eternity; then our salvation will be completed.

Salvation means being called by God. In past centuries of Baptist history disagreements over predestination have been quite severe. John Calvin's writings defined predestination and set the stage for centuries of debate. In the most extreme form, predestination teaches that God predetermined that certain persons would be saved and certain others would not be. Many who hold to this view have been strongly opposed to missions as presuming on God's sovereignty. The old arguments concerning predestination are rarely heard today. This makes it possible for us to examine the meaning of predestination in a more profitable way. Election is a doctrine that emphasizes the work of God in salvation. Words such as *predestined, called, chosen, elect,* and *foreknowledge* are used in the Bible to refer to God's action in salvation (see Mark 13:20; John 13:18; Rom. 8:29-30; Eph. 1:4; 1 Thess. 2:12; 2 Thess. 2:13; 1 Pet. 1:1-2). These terms and the contexts in which they appear sound very much like the choosing of Israel as the people of God, and that is exactly what God intended. As God chose Israel through no merit of her own, God chooses believers, the new Israel, through no merit of our own.

We can become caught up in the arguments about predestination and miss this central point: God took the initiative in salvation; He chose and called each believer personally. His offer of salvation is to everyone; His call is to the entire human race. When we witness, many respond to the call; when we do not, few respond. Thus, we are involved in sharing the call of God with the world. Does the fact that God's call is to everyone eliminate its significance? If all are called, is my call special? When you ask a group of believers to describe events leading to their salvation experiences, they will tell you how God used various events and experiences to bring them to the point of accepting Christ. Each believer may argue about election in the abstract, but few will argue against it in their own experiences. All of us feel that God moved personally to lead us to our salvation decisions.

But election to salvation is call with a purpose. The texts cited previously add such phrases as "to be holy and blameless" (Eph. 1:4), "to be conformed to the likeness of his Son" (Rom. 8:29), "to live lives worthy of God" (1 Thess. 2:12). Part of the glory of being chosen is that the God of the universe wants to use us in His work of redeeming the world. We are called into a new Kingdom, different from this world, with a different way of relating to God and persons, and with a different mission.

The apostle Paul had a sense of divine destiny. He believed that Jesus had saved him for a purpose, and he wanted to be everything that God had in mind when He touched him on the Damascus road. When Jesus laid hold of Paul, He broke the grip of the past, of sin and guilt, and commissioned him for a new life of service. We, too, are called to serve God. We must never forget that God has called us to be like Jesus in character and service.

Salvation means adoption. The New Testament uses a

number of different terms to describe the new relationship brought through Jesus' blood. *Adoption* is one of those. It not only describes salvation; it also describes a genuine relationship established through Christ. We are sons and daughters of God (see Rom. 8:15-17; Gal. 4:1-7). This new relationship is stated nowhere more clearly than in the Model Prayer. Addressing God as Father was a revolutionary idea. The Jews did not so much as pronounce God's name, much less call Him Father. The Old Testament sometimes refers to God as Father; but the idea is that He is Father of Israel. The term is not used to refer to an individual's relationship with God. In the New Testament, because of what Christ did, we can call God Father. In fact, *Abba,* the word Jesus used to refer to God, is actually a very intimate term like *daddy,* which is a more familiar and endearing name.

Adoption as children of God has enormous implications, and they are stated clearly in the New Testament (see Rom. 8:15-17). As adopted sons and daughters, we are co-heirs with Christ. We share in Christ's glory, whatever marvels that entails. Our adoption into God's family defines our salvation. We are sons and daughters of God. God relates to us as His own children. He teaches us; guides us; shapes us; molds us; uses us; blesses us; protects us; corrects us; and, as a divine parent, is pleased or grieved by our responses.

Salvation means union with Christ. Another key term that reflects a real experience that comes with salvation is *union with Christ.* John 14:20 states a powerful truth: "'On that day you will realize that I am in my Father, and you are in me, and I am in you.'" Paul referred numerous times to believers being in Christ (see Rom. 6:11; 8:1; 2 Cor. 5:17; Gal. 3:27; Eph. 2:10).

John 15:1-8 records Jesus' own description of this union as one of a vine with branches. We are joined with Christ; His life flows through us; from Him we receive our nourishment; we produce the fruits He would produce. This union with Christ involves all that the believer is and does; all of us become part of a living organism. Paul's statement in Galatians 2:20 demonstrates the depth and result of this union: "'I have been crucified with Christ and I no longer live, but Christ lives in me. The life I live in the body, I live by faith in the Son of God, who loved me and gave himself for me.'" This verse expresses the dynamic fact of the Christian's spiritual oneness with the risen Christ, which gives inexhaustible energy for carrying out God's purpose. God's power heals, redeems, cleanses, and forgives. It is a kindling energy that flows from the risen Christ into the hearts of His committed disciples.

Salvation: Saved and Secure

The term *eternal security* means the same as security of the believer. It does not mean that anyone who joins a church is secure. It is based on the biblical nature of salvation. I preached my first revival in East Tennessee, where I was raised. On several occasions I asked about the spiritual condition of certain individuals. I was told, "He professed the Lord" or "She professed the Lord." Then I asked if that person was attending church, living for the Lord, and serving Him. The answer was, "No, but he professed the Lord." After I received that answer about several men and women, I became weary of that word *professed*, because I realized that it had little meaning. Hebrews 4:14 exhorts us to "hold firmly to the faith we profess." "Hold firmly" means to cling tenaciously, get possession of, like a bulldog holding a rag.

When a person truly accepts Christ as Savior, he is given a guarantee that he will not again be lost (see John 3:36; 10:27-29; Phil. 1:5-6; 1 Pet. 1:5). Other texts call the believer's attention to the demand that he not be presumptuous about his salvation; those will be considered later. The truth of eternal security is a great comfort. Our salvation is not dependent on our own strength, but on God's. If it were dependent on us, most of us would be lost in the end. In giving us security, God does not violate our wills. As E. Y. Mullins stated, God "does not build walls so much as he builds wills."[1]

Genuine salvation is a life-changing experience. The person who truly experiences God's grace and commits his life to Jesus Christ will persevere. Because the believer has human weaknesses, he will have times of failure; but the true believer will sense God's disapproval of his wrongdoing and failure and repent of it. Deep within the heart of the true believer will be the desire to please God and have fellowship with Him.

Baptists reject the idea of falling from grace because that view does not acknowledge that God has the power to hold and keep His own. Baptists also reject the idea that if a person is saved, it makes no difference how he lives, since salvation is solely dependent on God. This view is false because it fails to acknowledge the enormous effect that salvation has on a person's life.

Eternal security must be interpreted in light of what the Bible teaches about salvation. Salvation is provided by God's grace. It brings forgiveness of sin and a new life in fellowship with God. That salvation is secure. It is given, sustained, and brought to completion by the grace of God. We are in God's hand, and His hand is very strong.

PERSONAL LEARNING ACTIVITY 6

On the lines below write your own testimony of salvation by completing the statements.

1. Before I met Christ, I _____

_____

_____

2. I experienced God's salvation when _____

_____

_____

3. Now that I have the gift of salvation, I _____

_____

_____

---

1. Edgar Young Mullins, *The Christian Religion in Its Doctrinal Expression* (Nashville: The Sunday School Board of the Southern Baptist Convention, 1917), 437.

CHAPTER 7

The Christian Life: Priests of God

You also, like living stones, are being built into a spiritual house to be a holy priesthood, offering spiritual sacrifices acceptable to God through Jesus Christ. You are a chosen people, a royal priesthood, a holy nation, a people belonging to God, that you may declare the praises of him who called you out of darkness into his wonderful light.
1 Peter 2:5,9

THE BIRTH OF A BABY IN A FAMILY IS a very important event. With the coming of a new life into a home, many changes take place. The love and care that mother, father, and brothers and sisters give to the little one take a lot of time and energy. It almost seems as if the entire family schedule is set by the baby. The baby must be fed, changed, loved, and cared for in every way. Everyone understands that this little newborn bundle of life is helpless. The baby requires total care for the first several months of its life. Even when the baby begins to grow and learn, it still has a long way to go before it is a full-grown, functioning human being. But growth is expected. That is the goal of life.

The newborn Christian, too, must grow. The experience of salvation—the new birth—is a life-changing event. It is a birth, the beginning of a new life. The new Christian is, in many ways, an infant. The goal for every newborn Christian is to become a mature, fully functioning disciple of Jesus. This means growth— growth in the Christian life.

The Bible has much to say about the Christian life. Christians have privileges, opportunities, and responsibilities. As a priest of

God, every believer has a ministry to perform. This makes it important for us to look to the Scriptures to find direction for growth in the Christian life.

The Christian Life: Priests and Temples of God

Christianity began as a lay movement. Even the leaders of the earliest church were laypersons, and all believers were encouraged to exercise their spiritual gifts as equals. As time went on, the church began to divide people into two classes, clergy and laity. This cleavage began to develop early in church history, and the rise of clericalism soon relegated the layperson to a spectator role in the ministry of the church.

This division between Christians is not biblical; all Christians are of one class before God. One cannot read Acts and passages like Ephesians 4:11-13 without recognizing that every Christian is a minister. This concept is at the heart of the New Testament doctrine of the priesthood of believers. Three of the main points of the doctrine of the priesthood of believers are: (1) the equality of all believers before God; (2) the right of each person to direct access to the Father; and (3) the responsibility of each believer for ministry, according to his gifts. This doctrine was revived during the Reformation, but the concepts were not fully developed at that time.

The priesthood of believers has always been important to Baptists. From our earliest history Baptists have insisted on every person's right of access to God and on every believer's responsibility to minister to others. This heritage has had a profound effect on every phase of Baptist life.

Following World War II a renaissance of the lay movement began. Writers from many different denominations and groups reminded us that it is not enough for laypersons simply to hand out church bulletins and pass the offering plates on Sunday morning.

Since all believers are called of God to ministry, the layperson cannot pay someone else to fulfill his or her ministry. Each person is accountable to God for the stewardship of personal spiritual gifts and cannot fulfill that God-given ministry by proxy.

A key passage that relates to the priesthood of believers is 1 Peter 2:9-10: "You are a chosen people, a royal priesthood, a holy nation, a people belonging to God, that you may declare the praises of him who called you out of darkness into his wonderful light. Once you were not a people, but now you are the people of God; once you had not received mercy, but now you have received mercy." This passage of Scripture provides a profound description of the people of God. Peter used Old Testament terms to describe the characteristics of New Testament saints. "A chosen people" refers to a selected race of an elected people. Just as God chose the Jews to be a light to the Gentiles, He chose the church, as a company of believers, to be His servant. A Christian is a part of a "royal priesthood," a people who are allowed to come into God's presence with petitions and sacrifices. God has called out Christians to form a "holy nation," a nation set apart for God's service. Paul used the descriptive phrase "a people that are his very own" (Titus 1:14) to indicate that God's people are uniquely His, to do His will and His work.

These terms, rooted in the Old Testament, are developed into their fullness in the New Testament. The truth that all believers are priests, each equal to every other, has been one of the most distinguishing doctrines of Baptists since our beginning. This doctrine has colored our interpretation of every other doctrine, and as we have developed our polity—our way of doing the work of our churches—the priesthood of believers has shaped our local church and denominational structure.

Essentially, every person who accepts Christ as Savior becomes a joint-heir with Jesus. This means that every believer is absolutely equal. The New Testament expresses this equality with the terms *priests* and *priesthood*. As brothers of Jesus, we are a kingdom (see Rev. 1:6; 5:10).

Our priesthood means that we represent God to people. Each of us is a bridge builder between God and persons as we minister and witness in His name. As priests, we can offer up sacrifices of our lives as we witness, praise, intercede in prayer, give, minister, visit, and help. Our priesthood also means that every believer can come before God on his or her own, without any other priest or intermediary of any kind except Jesus Christ Himself. That awesome privilege came about only because God made a new covenant with us through His Son. The entire Book of Hebrews emphasizes this right and privilege, asserting that we may come with confidence before the throne of grace (see Heb. 4:16).

Romans 12:1 has an unusual phrase that is difficult to translate: "spiritual worship." The Greek word translated as *worship* is *latreian*. It refers to carrying out religious rituals by the priests. There is no longer a sacrificial system. All of us believers are now priests, and the priestly work we do is sacrificing ourselves in the service of Christ, literally laying our bodies on the altar.

When we examine the many New Testament texts that reflect comparisons to the Jewish sacrificial system, the concept that all believers are priests is revealed as a dominant New Testament theme. The frequent reference to Christians as temples demonstrates that same truth. The people of God are referred to as temples in three ways in the New Testament: (1) the individual believer is a temple (see 1 Cor. 6:19); (2) a local church is a temple (see 1 Cor. 3:16-17); and (3) God's people all together are a temple (see Eph. 2:21).

The Greek word for the whole temple complex is *hieron;* the word for the holy of holies is *naos.* Not once is *hieron* used of believers; every time the word is *naos.* When the veil was torn in two from top to bottom (see Matt. 27:51) and the dividing wall of hostility was destroyed (see Eph. 2:14), two momentous results occurred: Not only was total and free access made possible for all who would believe, but also each believer became the special dwelling place of God. You and I are God's *naos,* the place where His presence dwells. The local church is God's *naos,* the place where His presence dwells. The people of God as a whole are God's *naos,* the place where His presence dwells. How poorly most of us reflect God's presence is a matter of shame, but the truth is there nonetheless. That is what God saved us to; that is what *priesthood of believers* means; that is what God holds us accountable for.

Peter expressed this truth by calling believers "living stones" being built into a "spiritual house" (see 1 Pet. 2:5). Paul used similar imagery in Ephesians 2:19-22. The Temple mount in Jerusalem is formed with huge rectangular stones. The Jewish historian Josephus recorded that Herod did not allow the sound of hammer or chisel in the Temple area. Every stone was shaped in the quarry to exact specifications for its place in the Temple. That is what Christ seeks to do with us. Each of us has a place in the spiritual house that Christ is building. By yielding to Him, by taking our priesthood seriously, we allow Christ to shape us until we fit His plan perfectly.

The Christian Life: Sanctification and Growth

Believers are described as "obedient children" in 1 Peter 1:14. We are never to stay as babes, but we do not skip the process of childhood as we grow in the Lord. First Peter 1:14-15 describes what obedience means: "Don't let your character be moulded by the desires of your ignorant days, but be holy in every part of your lives, for the one who has called you is himself holy" (Phillips).

Sanctification refers to the process of Christian growth. It means *to be set apart, to be holy.* Like *salvation,* the word actually has three aspects. We are sanctified (set apart) when we are first saved. Thus, every believer is a saint. If we are growing, we are constantly in the process of sanctification (being made holy). Finally, our sanctification will be completed (will be made holy) when we meet Christ in eternity. Baptists do not believe that anyone attains full sanctification (sinless perfection) in this life, though perfection is a goal for which we are to strive.

Matthew 6:33 commands, "'Seek first his kingdom and his righteousness, and all these things will be given to you as well.'" Jesus has priorities for the way we live our lives. So many things clamor for priority in our lives. We need to learn through the study of Scripture how to determine what is important in life. Life is more important than material possessions (see Luke 12:15). We are commanded to be strong in the power of God (see Eph. 6:10). We should live in awareness of our accountability to God (see Rom. 14:12).

Charles Sheldon's book *In His Steps* made a great impact on my life. I was overwhelmed by the concept of the question it asked, What would Jesus do? It inspired me to try to follow His example.

The goal of Christian living is beautifully expressed by Paul in Philippians 3:10-12: "I want to know Christ and the power of his resurrection and the fellowship of sharing in his sufferings, becoming like him in his death, and so, somehow, to attain to the resurrection from the dead. Not that I have already obtained all this, or have already been made perfect, but I press on to take hold of that for which Christ Jesus took hold of me." In this passage of Scripture Paul gives us our greatest reason for growing. You would think that after so many years of serving Christ, Paul would have had a complete understanding of Jesus and the Christian life. But he knew that growth is an ongoing process.

To know a person is much more than to know about him. To know about someone has value, but knowing has vitality. The verb *know* indicates knowledge grounded in personal experience. Phillips translates Paul's thought in verse 12, "trying to grasp that purpose for which Christ Jesus grasped me." To know Christ is to understand our purpose in the plan of God. Paul's desire was to fulfill everything that God had in mind for him to do when He saved him on the Damascus road.

Paul confessed that he had not reached full maturity. The *New International Version* uses the word *perfect* in verse 12. This is more clearly translated *full grown* or *mature*. Notice Paul's magnificent obsession in verses 13 and 14: "Brothers, I do not consider myself yet to have taken hold of it. But one thing I do: Forgetting what is behind and straining toward what is ahead, I press on toward the goal to win the prize for which God has called me heavenward in Christ Jesus." This kind of commitment brings maturity. It is developing, not remaining static, growing continually toward completion. Paul was caught up in the mission, the dream, and the vision God had given to him. He did not want to disappoint Jesus by failing to achieve the purpose for which he was saved. Like a runner in a race—the past was behind, and the finish line was ahead—Paul pressed forward to attain his goal.

Ephesians 1:15-20 records a beautiful prayer of Paul for the Ephesian Christians:

For this reason, ever since I heard about your faith in the Lord Jesus and your love for all the saints, I have not stopped giving thanks for you, remembering you in my prayers. I keep asking that the God of our Lord Jesus Christ, the glorious Father, may give you the Spirit of wisdom and revelation, so that you may know him better. I pray also that the eyes of your heart may be enlightened in order that you may know the hope to which he has called you, the riches of his glorious inheritance in the saints, and his incomparably great power for us who believe. That power is like the working of his mighty strength, which he exerted in Christ when he raised him from the dead and seated him at his right hand in the heavenly realms.

This prayer of Paul for the Ephesians includes some important requests that relate to all believers. First, Paul prayed that the Ephesian Christians have "the Spirit of wisdom and revelation" (v. 17). The Greek word for *wisdom* is *sophia*. This word refers to the practical understanding that comes as a gift of God. In the context of this verse it refers to understanding the revelation God has given of Himself.

Then Paul prayed that the eyes of their hearts be enlightened (v. 18). The heart signifies the inner being. The idea of the heart having eyes suggests that people need more than intellectual enlightenment. Inner realities can be grasped only by the heart; they can be seen only by the spiritual self. The realities that Paul wanted the Ephesians to see are "the hope to which he has called you, the riches of his glorious inheritance in the saints, and his incomparably great power for us who believe" (vv. 18-19). Paul did not explain what the hope to which we are called is, but the idea seems to be the total realm of spiritual attainment that God has made possible for us. The inheritance spoken of is the heritage of God's people, the overwhelming abundance of God's gifts to His people. The incomparable power referred to in verse 19 is the power of God that raised Jesus from the dead and exalted Him in heavenly places (see v. 20). The word for *power* in this verse is *dunamis*. It means *power, might, strength,* and *force*. Our English word *dynamite* comes from this word. The amazing truth is that this power is available "for us who believe" (v. 19).

The purpose for all that God has given is to fulfill His purpose in our lives. A phrase in verse 17 sums up the goal of Christian living: "so that you may know him better."

The Christian Life: the Call to Continued Growth

The Book of Hebrews warns of the dangers of not growing in Christ. Hebrews 3:13 instructs us to "encourage one another daily" to avoid this danger. The Christian must never take his relationship with God through Jesus for granted. We are not subject, if we are true believers, to losing our salvation, but we are subject to the terrible tragedy of missing God's will for our lives. Like the children of Israel, we may languish in the wilderness, though we are freed from the bondage of Egypt (see Heb. 3:8-9,15). This passage looks back to the rebellion of the Israelites at Meribah (Ex. 17:1-7), the place in the wilderness that marked forever the site of the Hebrews' rebellion against God.

The Israelites had a chance to inherit the Promised Land not long after they left Sinai. They sent spies into the land but became fearful and distrustful of God when the spies brought back their majority report. As a result, they languished in the wilderness for forty years, until all of the older, unbelieving, distrustful generation except for the two believers Caleb and Joshua died. The people's unbelief robbed them of the privilege of knowing God's will for their lives (see Deut. 1:26-36).

Hebrews 3:14 challenges us to hold firmly to the faith we had when we first walked with Jesus. This is a call to recover the joy of salvation.

Hebrews 5:11 to 6:3 is a call to spiritual maturity. The writer of Hebrews spoke of those who were "slow to learn" (v. 11), people so immature that they needed milk, not solid food (see v. 12). They were still infants so far as spiritual maturity was concerned (see v. 13). The people were not growing in Christ. They were not using their minds or their hearts. Some of these believers had been Christians long enough to have developed enough maturity to teach others, but they were in a constant process of recycling. A Christian today who neglects Bible study, prayer, and ministry has to recycle through the basic tenets of the faith to lay again a base that has eroded away because of disuse. Sanctification is not a matter of getting older; it is a matter of studying, praying, serving, and giving to the Lord. Paul struggled with this problem with the Corinthians (see 1 Cor. 3:2). Hebrews 6:1-2 emphasizes the importance of growth and development. Understanding what the Bible teaches about the key subjects is essential to good discipleship.

When a believer does not grow in Christ, he faces the serious danger of an ever-weakening faith. "See to it" (Heb. 3:12) could well be translated, "Look out," since the text cautions *believers* not to have evil, unbelieving hearts. "Turns away from" is the Greek word *aphistemi*, from which we get our word *apostasy*. That word has come to mean *losing one's faith*. However, the word in the first century meant moving away from one's faith. The readers were in danger of allowing the persecution to weaken their faith, and that weak faith would cause them to rebel, or step aside, from God.

The danger of backsliding is discussed further in Hebrews 6:4-10. *Enlightened* means *illumination;* here it refers to those who have come from darkness into light. If this text referred to the loss of salvation, it would teach that when a person fell from grace once, he never again had the possibility of salvation.

My counseling time is filled with the pain of Christian families torn apart because of the immorality of a spouse or of a son or a daughter. Many of these are Christians living outside the will of God, living as though they have no one to answer to or consider except themselves. Some of them have broken lives because of rebellion against God and family.

Fall away, parapesontas, means *to fall aside, to stand aside from.* A. T. Robertson insisted that the picture cannot be toned down because the Greek construction bluntly denies the possibility of renewal for apostates.[1] This is a difficult passage and can be dealt with only if it is taken in context with all of Hebrews. The book emphasizes the certainty of salvation because it is provided by Christ, who still lives and makes intercession for us. It is important, too, that we understand the probable historical context of the Book of Hebrews. It was a time of intense persecution in which people were pressured to deny Christ in order to save their lives. Those who denied Christ would be crucifying Him again because they would cast their lot with those who crucified Jesus, identifying themselves with His enemies. These unfaithful ones could not continue in the church. They had demonstrated that Jesus was not their Lord. Hebrews 6:9-12 clearly affirms the author's confidence in the salvation of his readers. Verses 4-6 must be interpreted in this context.

However, the text demonstrates that we seriously deny Christ when we backslide, when by life and word we deny the marvelous saving grace that Christ wrought in our lives. The writer enumerates the blessings and insights of faith: enlightenment, tasting heaven's gifts, sharing the power and presence of the Holy Spirit, tasting God's good Word, experiencing a taste of the powers of the coming age. To be unfaithful after experiencing those blessings is a terrible sin, and every believer must realize the extent of such guilt.

The great danger Hebrews focuses on in this text is being disqualified for service, not being usable in the kingdom of God. Paul spoke to this same problem in 1 Corinthians 9:24-27. He compared the Christian's life to the athlete who runs a race. His point, along with many other New Testament texts, is that perseverance is a valid test of salvation. The Hebrews text makes a different point with much the same effect, that the unfaithful Christian is on a collision course with disaster and must recommit his life to Christ and become reacquainted with His wonderful presence. Although he knew that his readers would not fall away (see Heb. 6:9; 10:38-39) because they were anchored in Christ Himself (see 6:17-20), he warned them not to take their salvation lightly.

The lives of these who have fallen away bring shame to Christ and His work of redemption. Their behavior in the light of the cross lifts Jesus up again naked and pierced, opens Him again to abuse and mockery. This text in Hebrews may contain the sharpest words given in the New Testament. God does not take lightly the behavior of Christians who bring Him such shame.

Hebrews 6:7-8 presents a contrast between land that produces a successful crop and land that produces only thorns and thistles. The lives of disobedient Christians present a picture to the world of a useless, thorn-infested field. This is a terrible denial of what it means to be a Christian.

A man was arrested by Hitler. His body was broken under extreme torture almost to the point of death, but the torturers could not break his spirit. Finally, he was sent to a concentration camp, where he languished in terrible conditions until he was liberated by the Allies. He came out with his hands, arms, and feet mutilated, but he came out with his head high because the Nazis could not break his spirit. A few months after he had been liberated, he found out that his own son had turned him in to the Gestapo. Within two weeks, he died of a broken heart. It was not the torment and torture of the enemy but rather the betrayal by his son that broke his spirit and led to his death. Certainly, our Lord Jesus Christ is humiliated before the world and crucified again by faithless Christians.

The writer of Hebrews made it clear to his readers that he did not expect them to fail in their Christian lives. He expressed confidence in them with these words: "Even though we speak like this, dear friends, we are confident of better things in your case—things that acccompany salvation" (Heb. 6:9). God calls us to responsible, fruitful living that evidences His work in our lives.

PERSONAL LEARNING ACTIVITY 7

All Christians are priests of God. Priesthood brings privileges and responsibilities. List some of each on the lines below.

Privileges of Priesthood	Responsibilities of Priesthood

---

1. Archibald Thomas Robertson, *Word Pictures in the New Testament*, vol. 5 (Nashville: The Sunday School Board of the Southern Baptist Convention, 1932), 375.

CHAPTER 8

The Christian Life: Living in the Spirit

"I will ask the Father, and he will give you another Counselor to be with you forever—the Spirit of truth. The world cannot accept him, because it neither sees him nor knows him. But you know him, for he lives with you and will be in you."
John 14:16-17

THE BELIEVER IS IN UNION WITH Christ. The Holy Spirit is the functioning agent of that union. Many Christians are not fully aware of all they have in Christ. Imagine for a moment that a woman lived in a very simple cottage that was comfortable but very ordinary. Then imagine that she discovered that the property on which the cottage stood was rich with gold. It had been there all along— just below the surface of the earth. The cabin owner was rich all the years she lived there. She just didn't know about her wealth. This situation illustrates many believers' relationship to the Holy Spirit. We have been given God's Spirit. We are rich, but many of us do not realize our wealth.

Every believer receives the Holy Spirit at the moment of conversion (see John 14:16-17; 1 Cor. 3:16; 6:19; 1 John 2:27). Many believers, either because they are not taught or because they do not hear what they are taught, are not aware of the presence of the Spirit. Some of them, when they later discover His power in their lives, wonder why they never heard that teaching before. The doctrine of the Holy Spirit is important. It has always been part of Baptist teaching. We will examine this important doctrine and discover the great wealth that is ours through the Spirit.

The Person of the Holy Spirit

The Holy Spirit is a Person, not an It. He is referred to by the pronoun *He* and is spoken of in terms of personality characteristics on numerous occasions in the New Testament. The Holy Spirit is often identified in the New Testament as the Spirit of Christ. References in Paul's writings reveal that Paul used terms about Jesus and about the Spirit interchangeably: "Now the Lord is the Spirit, and where the Spirit of the Lord is, there is freedom" (2 Cor. 3:17); "because you are sons, God sent the Spirit of his Son into our hearts" (Gal. 4:6). But even though the relationship between Christ and the Spirit is apparent, Christ and the Spirit are not identical. The Spirit is a separate Person. W. H. Griffith Thomas wrote: "Christ and the Spirit are different yet the same, the same yet different. Perhaps the best expression we can give is that while their Personalities are never identical, their presence always is."[1]

The Holy Spirit glorifies Christ. Jesus was quite clear about this work of the Spirit: "'When the Counselor comes, . . . he will testify about me'" (John 15:26); "'He will not speak on his own; he will speak only what he hears. . . . He will bring glory to me'" (John 16:13-14). This explains why we know so much more about the Person of Jesus than about the Person of the Holy Spirit. We hear from Jesus that the Spirit will come, and we read of the actions of the Spirit, but what we learn from the Spirit is about Christ. The focus of our prayers and worship is the Father and the Son. The Holy Spirit helps us pray, worship, and glorify Jesus. We must be cautious, however, not to think of the Spirit simply as Jesus in spirit form.

The Work of the Holy Spirit

What is the work of the Holy Spirit? What does He do in the life of the church and in the ongoing lives of individuals? The answer is many-faceted. We will look at some of these facets of truth concerning the Spirit. Because some of these truths have already been covered in previous chapters of this book, they will only be reviewed at this point. Others will be dealt with more extensively.

The Holy Spirit inspired the biblical writers. (See chap. 1.) The Bible is God's inspired Word. The Holy Spirit inspired the

INSPIRATION .
ILLUMINATION / REVELATION

human writers as they wrote it. Its content is authoritative and trustworthy. The Holy Spirit also inspires and illumines us as we study the Bible.

He leads to salvation. The Spirit convicts of sin, righteousness, and judgment (see John 16:8-11). His work is to lead persons to conviction of their sin, of their need for Christ's righteousness as their only hope, and of the fact of impending judgment if they do not repent.

He indwells the believer. The indwelling of the Holy Spirit is not an experience apart from salvation; every believer is indwelled by the Spirit at the moment of conversion (Rom. 8:9; 1 Cor. 12:3). This indwelling provides power and direction for life, provides guidance for developing as a disciple of Christ, and results in Christlike living.

He leads the church. The Book of Acts could be referred to as "The Acts of the Holy Spirit" rather than "The Acts of the Apostles." That title is more accurate. As we read Acts with the purpose of noticing the work of the Spirit, we are overwhelmed by the direction the Spirit gave to the early church. The Holy Spirit is an administrator. If we are open to His guidance and power, He reveals to us what gifts and ministries are needed, what fields of service to move into, and how to develop our gifts and ministries to prepare for entering those fields. In Acts 16 we read of Paul being forbidden by the Spirit to go to Bithynia. Instead, he was led by a vision to go to Macedonia. Looking back on this change of plans, Paul must have recognized the hand of God, since much of Paul's ministry took place after this time. His path would ultimately lead to Rome, where he would proclaim the gospel as a prisoner and write many of his letters. God knows what He is doing; we need simply to follow. The Spirit builds up the church, both in every local expression and in the fullness of the bride of Christ.

He is our counselor. The Bible speaks of the Holy Spirit as counselor (see John 14:16,26). The Greek word for *counselor, paraclete,* is sometimes used for *lawyer.* It means *one who walks alongside.* The Holy Spirit is with the believer always. He aids our ailing spirits and helps us through times of difficulty. He guides and directs us in making day-to-day decisions both great and small. Brother Payne, the mission pastor to a black congregation in Odessa, Texas, would often pray, "Lord, prop me up on my leaning side." This is a beautiful description of the word *paraclete*. Herschel H. Hobbs points out that Jesus is our advocate with God, while the Holy Spirit is God's advocate with us.[2]

He is our strength. The believer does not have to do the work of Christ in his own strength. The Holy Spirit provides the power for Christian life and service. It is in this context that some Christians discover the power of the Spirit. Having lived and worked in their own strength to the point of frustration and exhaustion, they finally discover that enormous power is available. The discovery leads to a new way of life. The power of the Spirit comes with salvation; unfortunately, many do not avail themselves of it.

The early Christians were so excited about their faith that, on one occasion, people thought they were drunk (see Acts 2:13). The "Jesus people" of the sixties and early seventies talked of being "high" on Jesus. The exhilaration is a wonderful experience, but it may or may not indicate being filled with the Spirit. The feeling is not an end in itself, and many who are filled with the Spirit do not feel a constant "high." The true test of the Spirit's power is whether the life is lived with power, joy, and surrender to God.

Part of this work of the Holy Spirit is to help us communicate with God. He leads us in prayer, and even when we do not know what to say, He still communicates our feelings that are so deep we do not even have clear thoughts about them (see Rom. 8:26-27).

He is our teacher. The Holy Spirit does not teach of Himself but of Christ (see 1 Cor. 12:3). The Spirit is our teacher as we seek to learn more of Christ, helping us understand who Christ is, the nature of His ministry, and His plans for the world. The more we learn of Christ, the more we see the world through His eyes and commit ourselves to be a part of His great work.

The Spirit teaches us, too, about how to live as Christ would have us live. This teaching is positive. We do not live Christlike lives unless we learn about Christ's attitude toward sin and its effect on people. Sometimes the Spirit leads us to oppose sins publicly and to seek to effect laws regulating them, as with gambling, alcohol, and abortion. He always leads us to address the sin problem by proclaiming a better way.

Part of this work of the Holy Spirit is to reveal to each of us what gift(s) He has given us and in what ministry the gift is to be used. Many Christians deny that they have gifts, but every believer is gifted. Every Christian is a minister, even though many do not understand that this is true.

He is our assurer. The believer's security is certain, and the Holy Spirit witnesses in our hearts to make us certain of that guarantee (see 2 Cor. 1:22; 5:5; Eph. 1:14). Most Christians go through periods when they doubt their salvation. Sometimes that is a healthy exercise, for doubt that plagues the mind needs to be surfaced and resolved. One of the blessings Christ gave us is the knowledge that Christ will keep us safe in salvation; the Spirit constantly confirms that truth in our lives so that we can live victoriously.

The Believer's Life in the Spirit

Paul discussed in Romans 7 the constant problem every believer has in daily living. In verses 1-13 Paul discussed the believer's relationship to the Old Testament law. The commandments of God served to identify sin and to bring the conviction of sinfulness. In Christ we have been set free from the devastating control of our sinful nature. We also have been set free from the tyranny of the law. We now belong to Christ and are able through Him to live lives of productive service (see vv. 4-6).

In Christ the victory is won, but the struggle continues. As believers we have a new nature; but we still have the sinful nature. Paul confessed his own struggle in verses 14-25. He experienced a constant conflict. Although he knew the right thing to do, he often found himself doing the opposite (see vv. 15,18,19). Paul summed up his situation in verse 20: "Now if I do what I do not want to do, it is no longer I who do it, but it is sin living in me that does it." Paul was not trying to deny responsibility for his actions. Rather, he recognized the struggle we all face, a struggle that we will always have as long as we live in this world.

Paul exclaimed in frustration: "What a wretched man I am! Who will rescue me from this body of death?" (Rom. 7:24). Then he gave the answer to his own question: "Thanks be to God—through Jesus Christ our Lord!" (Rom. 7:25).

Romans 8 speaks of the freedom from the power of sin that Christ has provided. The Old Testament law, Paul insisted, could not provide this freedom, because the sinful nature is unable to keep the law (see vv. 3-8). We cannot resist sin by seeking to follow an elaborate list of do's and don'ts. Those who seek to live by legalism have yet to discover that only Christ can set us free from the law of sin and death (see vv. 1-2). He does this for us through the indwelling Holy Spirit, who is able to live through us (see vv. 9-11). In the rest of Romans 8 Paul described the freedom we have in Christ. We have a new relationship reflected in the right Christ gave us to call God "'Abba, Father'" (see vv. 14-17). We can have victory even when we are suffering, for we know that God is working on a new creation in which we will have a part (see vv. 18-25). The Holy Spirit constantly is with us. He helps us in our weakness, helps us pray, intercedes for us, and gives us the strength to stay faithful to the salvation Christ has given us (see vv. 26-39).

The point of these chapters in Romans should not be missed. Every believer has the Holy Spirit's indwelling presence, but many believers live as though they were still in the flesh. These Scriptures exhort us to live in the Spirit. That is where freedom is.

Life in the power of the Spirit is a life of discipleship. Discipleship is not optional for the Christian. It is part of the experience of salvation. A disciple is a learner, a follower, one who seeks to be like the Master. We can be effective disciples only through the leadership and power of the Holy Spirit.

Several specific ingredients are essential for living as a disciple. Each of these is made possible through the work of the Holy Spirit in the believer's life. The first essential ingredient in discipleship is prayer. Any believer who feels that she does not need to pray should study the life of Jesus. If He needed to pray, how can any of us feel that we grow beyond it? Jesus taught us to approach God as a loving Father (see Luke 11:2). Jesus is our mediator.

We approach God through His merit. He intercedes for us at the right hand of the Father (see 1 Tim. 2:5; Heb. 1:3; 7:25). But there is more: The believer not only has a Father to whom he can pray and a Savior who intercedes for him. He also has the inner presence of the Holy Spirit, who reaches into the very depths of the human heart to aid in prayer (see Rom. 8:26-27).

Hebrews 4:16 is a remarkable verse about the prayer privilege of every believer. First, those who have believed can come into God's presence with boldness. "Let us draw near to God with a sincere heart in full assurance of faith" is the exhortation of Hebrews 10:22; the word *boldness* means *unstaggering confidence, openness, fearlessness.* We don't have to be afraid of God. We are not to come carelessly or flippantly; yet because of what Jesus did for us, we are part of God's family, and He will treat us as beloved children. Those who pray often find that the more they pray, the more at home they are with God and the more ease they feel in talking with God. Then we are told to come to the throne of grace, the throne room where Jesus is King of kings and Lord of lords, where He has judged and forgiven our sins. Jesus said that everyone who believes in Him " 'has eternal life and will not be condemned; he has crossed over from death to life' " (John 5:24). Jesus' throne room is not a judgment place but a forgiveness place. I do not enter the throne room as a condemned sinner but as a redeemed brother. Finally, we should come to Him when we need to feel pardon or purity or when we need assurance, comfort, or strength. We can go to Him with every need. He is there when we seek strength, knowledge, or direction. The Holy Spirit leads us in the priceless privilege of prayer.

The Holy Spirit leads us to obey. The call to obedience may seem at first glance to be a legalistic trap, a denial of freedom rather than a granting of it. Many New Testament texts deal with obedience and the results of the life that insists on freedom outside of Christ. There is no freedom outside of Christ, and those who seek to be free by directing their own lives find that they have become bound in slavery and have moved far away from the freedom they sought. The greatest freedom comes as we choose to do what God intends.

Hebrews 12:12-29 describes the dangers of not being obedient

to Christ. It describes the dangers of being careless and undisciplined, slipshod in spiritual life, inconsistent, and immature, all of which are the opposite of obeying. Jesus was obedient
unto death, and we are to give that same kind of obedience to His
Word (see John 8:31-32). The will of Jesus is to be owned and
honored as the law of the Christian's life. The question comes,
How are we to know what He wants us to do so that we may obey
Him? One answer to that question is that we have the Bible to
instruct us. The Holy Spirit inspired the writing of the Scriptures, and they give us directions for successful living (see
2 Tim. 3:16). A second answer to the question of how we can
know the will of God is that we are led into truth by the Holy
Spirit (see John 14:26). The Spirit takes the teachings of Scripture and life's circumstances and brings them together. We can
find inner direction to understand what God wants for us in every
situation. We find also the inner strength to obey God through
the power of the Spirit.

The Holy Spirit leads us to discover our spiritual gifts. The
truth that each believer is gifted is an important teaching of the
New Testament. Three chapters list New Testament gifts: Romans 12; 1 Corinthians 12; and Ephesians 4. These lists overlap,
and they do not represent all the gifts the Spirit gives and uses,
but a study of them demonstrates the diversity and the need for
all of God's gifts.

What is the purpose of the spiritual gifts? The clearest answer
to that question is found in 1 Corinthians 12. As Paul wrote to
the Corinthians, who seemed to take personal pride in their gifts,
he made it clear that the gifts are given for service and ministry
(see 1 Cor. 12:4-6). They also are intended to benefit and build
up the church, the body of Christ (see 1 Cor. 12:7). The Scriptures do not even suggest that spiritual gifts are given for personal pleasure or for boastful purposes.

Each believer is given a spiritual gift (see 1 Cor. 12:7). Some
believers are blessed with multiple gifts. These gifts are from the
Holy Spirit. He is their source, and He gives them according to
His plan (see 1 Cor. 12:11). Only the Spirit can reveal our gift or
gifts to us and empower us to use them for the glory of God and
the good of the church.

The Fruit of the Spirit

Just as the gifts of the Spirit equip the Christian for service, the fruit of the Spirit gives meaning to Christian living. Galatians 5:22-23 provides a description of the fruit of the Spirit: "The fruit of the Spirit is love, joy, peace, patience, kindness, goodness, faithfulness, gentleness and self-control. Against such things there is no law." In the verses just before these, Paul had listed what he called the acts of the sinful nature (see Gal. 5:19-21). It is not an attractive list. It includes the most destructive and evil acts and emotions imaginable. The contrast between the acts of the sinful nature and the fruit of the Spirit is stark. Evil has as its source the worst in human nature. On the other hand, the positive redemptive qualities included in the fruit of the Spirit have as their source the Holy Spirit.

Another contrast is found in the fact that evil is the result of many acts, plural, while good is just one fruit, singular. There is only one source of good. That source is God. The fruit has several manifestations; but it is all the fruit of the Spirit. This suggests that only the Spirit can produce the good qualities listed in Galatians 5:22-23. They do not grow out of human effort. They are produced from within by the Holy Spirit, just as the fruit on a healthy tree comes from the vitality and life of the tree. The truth is that if the fruit of the Spirit characterizes our lives, it will have to be produced from within by God's Spirit. The work of the Spirit in the Christian's life will manifest itself in the fruit of the Spirit.

What are the manifestations of the fruit of the Spirit? In these verses Paul provided a list of these beautiful traits that characterize a Spirit-controlled life. The first is love. The Greek word is *agape,* the word used in the New Testament to describe God's kind of love. God's love places great value on persons and cares for them, even to the point of great sacrifice. It is a love that never fails and never ends (see 1 Cor. 13:8). It is a redemptive love that will not give up. Many shades and kinds of love operate in human experience. We often use the word *love* with little depth of meaning. But the Spirit produces the fruit of *agape* in believers. This is not natural or normal for us. It does not come from our own human nature. It is created from within us by the Holy Spirit.

The second quality of life that the Spirit produces in us is joy. The Greek word is *chara*. This word is from the same root as *charis*, the beautiful word that we translate *grace*. This joy is far more than the momentary periods of happiness that all human beings experience. It is a gift that issues in a life of goodwill, generosity, and gladness. This joy is also forgiving and overcoming, even in the face of rejection and in the worst of circumstances. It is an uncomparable gladness that accepts no barriers. Such joy can be ours only as it is created from within by the Holy Spirit. I have seen Christians express this joy at the most trying times. It is not created by human power, and it cannot be destroyed by human difficulty.

The third expression of the fruit of the Spirit is peace. *Peace* is a translation of the Greek word *eirene*, which means *total well-being*. It carries the idea of right relations with God and justice among people. The fruit of peace does not bring immunity from strife and storms. It is much more than an escape from trouble. It is a guard for the heart and the mind that goes beyond human understanding (see Phil. 4:7). It is the peace promised by Jesus, a peace the world cannot give, a peace that overcomes trouble and fear (see John 14:27).

The next characteristic of the fruit of the Spirit is patience. The Greek word is *makrothumia*, which carries the idea of being under control. It is not stoic, nor is it hopeless resignation. It is patience that works toward a goal or a purpose. The Holy Spirit creates this quality within Christians, making life purposeful and effective.

Kindness is an expression of the fruit of the Spirit, also. The Greek word, *chrestotes*, means *goodness, honesty,* and *kindness.* This Christlike quality of relating to others is created in Christians by the Holy Spirit.

Goodness translates *agathosune*. Paul used the word when he expressed confidence that the Roman Christians were "full of goodness" (Rom. 15:14). It means *righteousness* and *kindness*, as well as *goodness*. The idea is one of positive, active goodness.

Another trait of the Christian character produced by the Holy Spirit is faithfulness. The Greek word is *pistis*. This word means both *faith* and *faithfulness*, but *faithfulness* is better in this context. It is really faith that has been activated by love. Paul is a good example of this quality. His faith in Christ led him to a steadfast faithfulness to Christ. This was demonstrated over and over again in the long years of Paul's ministry. When he was saying farewell to his friends in Ephesus, Paul expressed this attitude of faithfulness: "'I consider my life worth nothing to me, if only I may finish the race and complete the task the Lord Jesus has given me'" (Acts 20:24). Paul's faith expressed itself in faithfulness. This quality, given by the Spirit, keeps Christians steady as they serve Jesus through the changing days.

Gentleness is from the Greek word *prautes*. It is the word translated *meek* in "'Blessed are the meek, for they will inherit the earth'" (Matt. 5:5). It is also the word applied to Jesus when He said, "'I am gentle and humble in heart'" (Matt. 11:29). It has to do with modesty and courtesy. The gentle person will not be arrogant and boastful. Rather, he will have a proper sense of self and will act graciously toward others. It is not weakness. On the contrary, great strength lies in gentleness. The Holy Spirit produces this quality in the lives of believers.

The final evidence of fruit listed by Paul is self-control. The Greek word is *egkrateia*. It is sometimes translated *temperance*, but its meaning is broader than that. It has to do with self-mastery. It is not to be understood in a stoic sense. Self-control is not an end in itself. In the sense that Paul understood it, it was life under the control of Christ (see Gal. 2:20). This disciplined kind of living is generated and sustained by the Holy Spirit.

At the conclusion of this list of the fruit of the Spirit, Paul added, "Against such things there is no law" (Gal. 5:23). How could there be any law against this kind of living? Yet we must remember that these traits of living describe the kind of life Jesus lived; and He was hated and opposed by the forces of evil. Paul did not imply, then, that Spirit-controlled living will make the Christian immune to opposition. He did point to this kind of living as positive and redemptive. No legitimate fault can be found with Christlike living.

The fruit is "of the Spirit." It is supernatural. It is not created by human effort but by the Holy Spirit's miraculous power. The believer's part is to submit to the Spirit's control.

PERSONAL LEARNING ACTIVITY 8

Concerning the qualities the Bible calls the "fruit of the Spirit," the author says: "They do not grow out of human effort. They are produced from within by the Holy Spirit, just as the fruit on a healthy tree comes from the vitality and life of the tree." On the tree below list the manifestations of the "fruit of the Spirit" found in Galatians 5:22-23. Beneath each fruit on the tree write a synonym for the name you have listed.

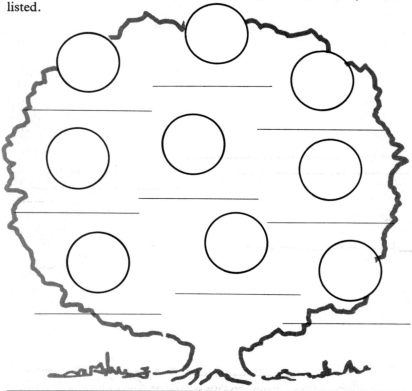

1. W. H. Griffith Thomas, *The Holy Spirit of God* (Grand Rapids: Wm. B. Eerdmans Publishing Company, 1955), 144.
2. Herschel H. Hobbs, *Fundamentals of Our Faith* (Nashville: Broadman Press, 1960), 61.

CHAPTER 9

The Church

Simon Peter answered, "You are the Christ, the Son of the living God." Jesus replied, "Blessed are you, Simon son of Jonah, for this was not revealed to you by man, but by my Father in heaven. And I tell you that you are Peter, and on this rock I will build my church, and the gates of Hades will not overcome it."
Matthew 16:16-18

ONE OF THE MOST DRAMATIC events of all time took place at a place called Caesarea Philippi. Jesus asked His followers the question "'Who do people say the Son of Man is?'" (Matt. 16:13). The disciples gave various answers: John the Baptist, Elijah, Jeremiah, one of the prophets. There must have been a lot of speculation about Jesus. Everyone seemed to be talking about Him. Then Jesus asked the really pertinent question: "'But what about you?' he asked. 'Who do you say I am?'" (Matt. 16:15). Peter answered for the group, "'You are the Christ, the Son of the living God'" (Matt. 16:16). We often refer to Peter's statement as the great confession. So far as we know from the Scripture, this was the first time the disciples had confessed Jesus as the Christ. Jesus' response was enthusiastic: "'Blessed are you, Simon son of Jonah, for this was not revealed to you by man, but by my Father in heaven. And I tell you that you are Peter, and on this rock I will build my church, and the gates of Hades will not overcome it'" (Matt. 16:17-18). In this statement to Peter, Jesus spoke of His church for the first time. The word *church* is a translation of the Greek word *ekklesia*. This word, which appears more than one hundred times in the New Testament, refers to an assembly that has been gathered for a specific purpose. It was often used to

111

refer to the political assembly in a Roman city-state. When used in the New Testament, it refers to the called-out ones, those who have been summoned by God to worship and serve Christ.

NOTE What was the rock on which Jesus promised to build His church (see Matt. 16:18)? This question has been the focus of much discussion among Christians. Some claim that Peter is the rock on which Jesus built His church. Baptists and other Protestant Christians do not accept this interpretation. Others have found significance in a play on words. The Greek word translated *Peter, petros,* refers to a small stone used in building. When Jesus said that He would build His church on a rock, He used the word *petra,* which refers to a large cliff or foundation stone. Those who hold to this interpretation believe that it points to Christ as the foundation stone on which the church is built, and to Peter, along with all other believers, as the smaller stones that make up the church. One problem with this interpretation is that Aramaic, the language of Jesus, did not have these two distinctive words. Thus, Jesus could not have used this play on words when He spoke these words originally.

A better interpretation looks at the confession of Peter, the truth that Jesus is the Christ, as the rock on which Jesus determined to build His church. The church is built on the reality of Christ's sonship, and those who accept the truth about Him make up His church.

Most significantly, the church Jesus built would be His church: "'I will build my church'" (Matt. 16:18). The church is His, not ours. We must never forget that the church belongs to Jesus.

The Church: Local and Universal

The Baptist Faith and Message says this about the church: "A New Testament church of the Lord Jesus Christ is a local body of baptized believers who are associated by covenant in the faith and fellowship of the gospel." Later in its statement about the church *The Baptist Faith and Message* says, "The New Testament speaks also of the church as the body of Christ which includes all of the redeemed of all the ages."

Two related but distant uses of the word *church* are found in the

New Testament. Herschel H. Hobbs points out that the New Testament uses the word *church* to refer to a local body of believers ninety-three times.[1] This means that in most New Testament passages the church is depicted as a local assembly of Christians who meet, worship, and minister in the name of Jesus Christ. A local congregation under the lordship of Christ is the only tangible expression of the church. The word *church* is never used in the New Testament in the singular to refer to a denomination or to a group of churches. Therefore, it is not correct to speak of "the Baptist church" when referring to the denomination. When the New Testament refers to groups of churches, it always uses the word in the plural (see Gal. 1:2).

Even though *church* usually refers to a local assembly, the word is also used in a more universal and general sense. When Jesus said, "'I will build my church'" (Matt. 16:18), He was obviously using the word in a sense that is broader than a local group of believers. The same is true in Ephesians 5:25. Here we are told, "Husbands, love your wives, just as Christ loved the church and gave himself up for her." The church for which Jesus gave Himself is something bigger than a local congregation. These are two examples of the church as the larger community of Christians. All believers of all time are part of the church in this sense. A brotherhood and sisterhood of Christians exists, crossing all barriers of race, geography, tradition, and denomination.

The Church: a Believers' Church

Acts 2:42-47 gives Luke's summary of God's work in the lives of His people in the earliest days of the Jerusalem church. Verse 47 is particularly significant: "The Lord added to their number daily those who were being saved." Notice that it was the Lord who was adding people to the church. Notice, too, that those added were the saved, that is, those who believed and as a consequence of their belief were baptized (see Acts 2:38). The church, then, is made up of believers in Jesus Christ. Only believers are part of God's church in the larger sense. Only believers are fit subjects for membership in a local church. Only believers are proper candidates for baptism. Philip baptized the Ethiopian only after he believed in Christ (see Acts 8:36-37).

membership

Infants are not proper subjects for baptism and church membership. The very nature of faith precludes any person's making a faith decision for another. Faith is a personal decision, or it is not faith at all. No one may be a believer unless he or she decides personally to believe. The goal of Baptists always has been that the church should be made up only of believers. Thus, baptism is impossible for infants. We cannot make decisions concerning faith in Christ for members of our family.

In the term *believers' church* note the placement of the apostrophe. The church is not *a* believer's church, but it is a community of believers. Further, the community gathers together in covenant. That is, each member covenants with God and with other members to live out faithfully the beliefs, practices, and mission of the body. Sometimes our evangelistic techniques overlook the covenant nature of a church by not explaining to the newly evangelized the nature of the church relationship. New member and counseling orientation at the point of decision are major ways to rectify this problem; but whatever the method, churches very much need to recover the sense of community by teaching their people the nature of church membership, commitment, and participation.

The community-in-covenant concept, as is true of so much of Baptist faith and practice, is based on the priesthood of believers. W. A. Criswell in *The Doctrine of the Church* clarified this concept well.

Despite the diversity in gifts and functions, the church is one body, and all its members have the same relationship to Christ. Access to God's presence was once the exclusive privilege of priests. It still is. But the change is that believers are made priests unto God and enjoy direct access through Christ's death and resurrection (Rom. 5:1-2; Rev. 1:5-6) so that priesthood now includes all believers. . . .

The belief that every believer is a priest is functional in Baptist worship services, church government, and ministry. One is asked to "lead the congregation in prayer"; thus, the congregation prays for all the requests. As many members as possible participate in the services, and the whole congregation normally sings and reads the Bible together as an act of corporate worship. . . .

Every member shares in the formulation of policies for the local church so that it is not subject to the authority of any external body.[2]

The Church: Biblical Pictures

We can understand the nature of the church better if we examine some of the figures or pictures used in the Bible to illustrate the church.

The church is the body of Christ. The human body is one of the most awe-inspiring of all God's creations. It is one of Paul's favorite analogies of the church (see 1 Cor. 12:12-27; Eph. 1:22-23; 2:16; 4:4,12,16; 5:23,30; Col. 1:18,24; 2:19; 3:15). In his book *The Nature of the Church* Bill J. Leonard suggests that the designation of the church as the body of Christ is important for several reasons. First, if the church is the body of Christ, that means that Christ's own presence is in the life of His church. It indicates a direct and intimate relationship between Christ and His church. Second, the idea of the church's being the body of Christ speaks to the unity of the church. As the body has an essential unity, so does the church (see 1 Cor. 12:12). Those related to Christ are also related to one another. A third implication of the church's being the body of Christ is that Christ is the head of the body, His church (see Col. 1:18). Since Christ is the head of the church, He gives it purpose and unity.[3]

The church functions most effectively when it has the use of all its parts (1 Cor. 12:21,24-25). This is a picture of unity in diversity. Paul indicated that this solidarity transcends all race and class distinctions as people merge into the body of Christ. People are not to be considered "Jew nor Greek, slave nor free, male nor female, for you are all one in Christ Jesus" (Gal. 3:28).

The church is referred to as the people of God. One passage of Scripture that carries this image is 1 Peter 2:9-10: "You are a chosen people, a royal priesthood, a holy nation, a people belonging to God, that you may declare the praises of him who called you out of darkness into his wonderful light. Once you were not a people, but now you are the people of God; once you had not received mercy, but now you have received mercy." This image reaches back to the Old Testament understanding of Israel as the people of God. The church is God's new people. This designation of the church as the people of God identifies the church as the special possession of God, in the world to do His work. God is building His people into a spiritual house. Our purpose is to serve God by giving ourselves to Him as a spiritual sacrifice (see 1 Pet. 2:5).

III. ***The church is called the family of believers or members of God's household.*** (See Gal. 6:10; Eph. 2:19.) This image of the church involves the relationship between God and His people and the relationship that exists between brothers and sisters in the church. God is Father in the most intimate sense (see Gal. 4:6-7). We are His children (see Rom. 8:16-17). We are brothers and sisters in Christ. As such, we are to love one another (see 1 John 3:11).

IV. ***The church is the bride of Christ.*** (See 2 Cor. 11:2; Rev. 19:7-9; 21:9; 22:17.) The idea of the church as Christ's bride is an appealing one. It suggests loving care on the part of Jesus for His church. Ephesians 5:22-32 seems to suggest this idea, as Paul commands husbands to love their wives "just as Christ loved the church." Revelation 19:7-9 describes a coming marriage feast for Christ and His church at the end of time, which is a picture of great victory and joy.

V. ***The church is an expression of the kingdom of God.*** The kingdom is the rule of Christ in the hearts of people. The church is the kingdom of heaven on earth in the sense that it is made up of people who have yielded their lives to Christ's rule. The concept recognizes that Jesus is King and His people are His subjects, and it recognizes that believers are citizens of another kingdom more important, stronger, and more lasting than any secular kingdom or nation that seems to have enormous and overwhelming power (see Col. 1:13). In the Model Prayer (Matt. 6:9-13) the first thing for which the believer is instructed to pray, after praising God, is for God's kingdom to come on earth as it is in heaven.

The Church Ordinances   vs "SACRAMENTS"

What is the nature of baptism and the Lord's Supper? Baptists reject the idea that baptism and the Lord's Supper are sacraments through which the church dispenses grace, taking them instead to be symbolic. Grace is conferred directly from Christ to the believer. There is no intermediary of any kind, whether priest or substance. Baptists refer to baptism and the Lord's Supper as ordinances. The word *ordinance* means that which is ordered, set out, decided, marked off, or put in place. An ordinance is a command that has purpose and meaning. The ordinances of baptism and the Lord's Supper are important parts of Baptist life. The Jews used water for purposes of religious purification. One specialized use of water among the Jews was for proselyte baptism. A proselyte was a Gentile who had converted to the Jewish faith. Such persons were baptized to symbolize religious purification and dedication to God. The Old Testament contains no reference to proselyte baptism, but other Jewish writings indicate that it was practiced as early as the first century AD. John took the practice and added another dimension to it. To become spiritually clean, he preached, one must repent in preparation for the coming of God's kingdom. His baptism followed the decision to repent and indicated publicly that the decision was made (see Matt. 3:1-6).

Jesus' baptism (see Matt. 3:13-17) established the importance of baptism. Why was Jesus baptized? What does "'fulfill all righteousness'" mean? First, Jesus was baptized to identify with sinful humanity. Second, He set an example. Early followers took the example seriously. Third, Jesus was announcing the beginning of His ministry. Fourth, Jesus was identifying His ministry with John's. John proclaimed that the kingdom was coming. Jesus' baptism made clear that the kingdom John prophesied had come in Him. Moreover, repentance is a central part of the message of Jesus, as it was of John's. Jesus would not act in a way that would imply that salvation is possible without repentance.

Baptists sometimes are accused of minimizing the importance of baptism because we do not believe that it is essential for salvation. Nothing could be further from the truth. The commandment to be baptized is so clear that no one can misunderstand it, and it is inconceivable that anyone truly saved would refuse to follow this first command of our Lord.

Baptism is a picture; in fact, it is several pictures. First, it pictures the death, burial, and resurrection of Christ. Second, it pictures the believer's death to sin and resurrection to new life in Christ. Third, it pictures union with Christ; immersion in the name of the Triune God indicates a new life in Christ (see Rom. 6:4; Gal. 3:27). Fourth, it pictures union with the people of God (see 1 Cor. 12:13). When a believer is baptized, he witnesses to a belief in what Christ has done in his life (see Col. 2:12), commits to live in union with Christ, and commits to being part of the church, the people of God.

If baptism pictures these four things, then it has meaning only if the person being baptized understands its meaning. Baptists believe in the baptism of believers and only believers. Baptism has absolutely no value to an infant, to a child under the age of accountability, or to any person who has been manipulated into making a decision without understanding. Under such conditions, the persons have not been baptized but only dipped in water. Understanding faith in Jesus Christ as Lord and Savior is essential prior to baptism.

Baptists have been firm in their position that the only proper mode of baptism is immersion. We must root our convictions in the Bible and the Bible only. The Greek word *baptizo* means *immersion;* it does not mean anything else. Of even greater importance is the fact that only immersion can picture the death, burial, and resurrection of Christ or the believer's dying to sin and rising to new life.

If baptism is not essential to salvation, why make such stringent requirements? The reason is that the doctrine of baptism is worth protecting. It is for believers only; it is to be by immersion only; it is not necessary for salvation; it is an ordinance of the church and not of the individual. Only by holding on to these principles strongly can the doctrine of baptism, as the Bible teaches it, survive.

Baptists sometimes refer to the ordinance of the Lord's Supper as communion. Paul wrote to the Corinthians: "Is not the cup of thanksgiving for which we give thanks a participation in the blood of Christ? And is not the bread that we break a participation in the body of Christ?" (1 Cor. 10:16). This verse does express the communal nature of the supper. But the Lord's Supper is more properly called a Memorial Supper. The institution of the ordinance is recorded in all four Gospels (Matt. 26:26-29; Mark 14:22-25; Luke 22:17-20; less clearly in John 13) and in 1 Corinthians 11:23-25. The stated purpose is to remind Jesus' disciples through the ages of Jesus' atoning death. The bread represents Jesus' body that was broken, and the cup represents His blood that was shed. This ordinance is to be observed until Christ returns.

The Lord's Supper in the New Testament parallels the Old Testament Passover. Jesus made this clear by instituting it at the Passover season. The deliverance from Egypt was celebrated by the Passover; the great deliverance from the slavery of sin is celebrated by the Lord's Supper.

Who is invited to observe the Lord's Supper in Baptist churches? Baptists do not speak with one voice in answering this question. Some churches feel that only the members of that local *"CLOSED"* congregation should participate in the supper. This view is strongly influenced by the Landmark tradition. Most who hold this view would point out that only members are subject to the discipline of a local congregation. Therefore, only members should come to the Lord's table.

Other churches invite members of sister Baptist churches to *"CLOSE"* participate. Others include those who come from churches that practice believer's baptism by immersion. Many Baptist churches invite all believers in Christ to come to the Lord's table. These churches accept individual faith in Christ as the main criterion for observing the ordinance. Paul said to the Corinthian church, "A man ought to examine himself before he eats of the bread and drinks of the cup" (1 Cor. 11:28). Churches that prac- *"OPEN"* tice a more open observance of the Lord's Supper leave that examination to the individual Christian.

Churches observe the ordinance with different frequencies, some once each month, most quarterly, a few less often. The Bible does not tell us how often to observe this memorial, but it should be often enough to keep Christ's atonement before us and not so often as to become commonplace. It is most effective when a worship service is built around it, making it an opportunity for reaffirmation, as well as for evangelism.

The Church: Officers and Ministries

The Baptist Faith and Message identifies two officers of the church: pastor and deacon. Southern Baptists have reemphasized the ministry of the laity through various efforts: doctrine studies on the laity (*The Doctrine of the Laity*), Shared Ministry, The Year of the Laity, gift discovery, and other efforts to call all of God's people to their appointed ministries. Those efforts attempt to reaffirm the role in ministry laypersons have had from the beginning and throughout Baptist history. The emphasis on laity in no way diminishes the roles of the pastor and the deacon; it does, however, speak to the nature of those roles.

The pastor is the leader of the church. Such New Testament pasages as 1 Timothy 5:17-19 and 1 Peter 5:1-5 affirm this fact. The question is not whether he is the leader, but what the nature of that leadership is. Ephesians 4:11-12 provides the answer. The pastor (alongside apostles, prophets, and evangelists) is to prepare God's people for works of service. The pastor is God's undershepherd, called by God to equip His people. How he goes about this equipping task is a matter of leadership style, but the style should be compatible with the work of equipping. Equipping should be central in all he does. He leads the church because the church calls him to do so. The pastor should lead with prayerful humility. The respect he receives from his people results from his Christlike living. W. A. Criswell advises pastors, "Don't become so dictatorial that you lord it over God's people and God's heritage." He further admonishes, "Don't forget that you are a servant."[4] The pastor is the leader of the church.

The work of the deacon is not so clearly described. *Deacon*, from *diakonos*, means *servant*. As the New Testament period progressed, the office of deacon evolved, but we cannot determine what particular responsibilities were attached to it. In fact, it is quite possible that the office held no specific duties but rather that the deacon served in whatever areas were needed.

Some believe that the first reference to the deacon may be Acts 6:1-6, the well-known account of selecting seven men to administer the daily distribution of food to the Greek-speaking widows who were being neglected. The word *deacon* is not used in this passage in reference to the seven men, but many believe that the office evolved from this early beginning. Possibly, the office of deacon evolved over a number of years; at any rate, by late in the New Testament period, the office of deacon had emerged alongside that of the pastor (see Phil. 1:1; 1 Tim. 3:1-13).

The question of the deacon's responsibilities, however, cannot be answered with certainty. The word itself provides some guidance. Its meaning stipulates ministry, which covers a wide range of activities. The New Testament does not support the idea of deacons as a board of directors who run the church. As spiritually mature individuals who have been elected by the church, the deacons are involved in leadership and ministry. The deacons move outside the New Testament office, however, when they assume power. They can minister in many ways: planning, counseling the pastor and one another, resolving crises, reconciling, supporting church programs, and modeling churchmanship.

A Baptist church performs many ministries. Because the pastor and deacons cannot do them all, many volunteer ministers are needed. These include teachers, leaders, and workers in Sunday School, Church Training, music, and missions, plus many committee positions. In addition, a church staff may have one or many paid ministers, depending on the size and the ministry of the church. A church is accountable to Jesus Christ to use every gift at its disposal, and each member is accountable to find his gift and to use it in ministry. The church is under obligation to call out the gifts of its members, equip them, and channel them into ministries in which they may use their gifts faithfully.

The Church: Purposes of the Church

The church belongs to Jesus. It is in the world to accomplish His purposes. These purposes define the nature and the work of the church. We will look briefly at some of these reasons for the church's existence.

Worship is a primary purpose of the church. Walter T. Conner wrote, "The first business, then, of a church is not evangelism, nor missions, nor benevolence; it is worship."[5] He went on to explain that worship is the mainspring of all else a church does; it provides the church's direction as people praise God and listen to the voice of Christ. The activist mentality of Southern Baptists *NOTE:* does not preclude genuine worship, but it requires discipline, lest a worship service become little more than a time of promoting activities and emphases. True worship includes the total person, both mind and emotion, in a way that calls him or her to praise God for who He is and what He has done and, in so doing, to reach new awarenesses, to learn more of God. When we read the passages in Revelation that describe life around God's throne, we come to a conviction that worship of God is what we were created for.

2. *Proclamation is* another purpose of the church. Just prior to His ascension, Jesus spoke these words to His disciples: "'You will receive power when the Holy Spirit comes on you; and you will be my witnesses in Jerusalem, and in all Judea and Samaria, and to the ends of the earth'" (Acts 1:8). We refer to this and the related passage in Matthew 28:18-20 as the Great Commission, the mandate of Jesus for His church. Proclamation of the gospel to all people everywhere is not an option. It is the very center of what a church is all about.

At least five elements of mission are included in the Great Commission. The first element is witnessing. God's plan is that those who have accepted His love and have believed on Jesus are to be living evidence of their salvation and that life is to include verbal witnessing (see Acts 5:32).

The second part of our mission is to see the need. We must see the crowds as Jesus saw them. Jesus looked at people with compassion, for He saw them as sheep without a shepherd (see Matt. 9:36). Unless we care deeply for people, we will not be effective witnesses.

The third matter we need to consider about witnessing relates to the places of mission. There is no boundary that Jesus does not cross, no people or land or culture that He does not want us to penetrate. He wants us to go everywhere human beings exist.

In the fourth place, Jesus sends us with power. He promised His followers, "'You will receive power when the Holy Spirit comes on you'" (Acts 1:8). This power for proclamation guarantees effectiveness. Mary Slessor was a young Scottish girl who went to Africa as a pioneer missionary. She worked primarily with men to reach the tribes. One day she told a chief who had become a Christian: "Here is what God wants us to do. He wants us to take this whole tribe for Christ. Then he wants us to go to the next tribe, and tribe by tribe God wants us to spread over Africa. My prayer is we will reach Africa for Christ out of this tribe that has come first to know Christ."

The chief listened to her plans and replied: "You can't do all of that. You are only a woman."

She said, "Yes, I am only a woman, but have you forgotten what kind of God this woman has?"

Finally, the task of proclamation requires that we speak as we go. Jesus commanded His disciples, "'Therefore go and make disciples of all nations'" (Matt. 28:19). A very literal translation of this verse is, "Going, therefore, disciple all the nations." The idea is to witness as we go. The task is too urgent to wait for the perfect time. Keith Parks has related an experience when he was working for the Lord in Indonesia. He lived on a major thoroughfare that in those earlier days was unpaved. The dust from the passersby was terrible. One day when the wind was blowing the other way, he was studying the Bible on the side of the street. As he watched the teeming multitudes of people moving on that road, he decided to count them. He tried, but he could not count fast enough. The weight of the numbers began to oppress his soul, and he cried out to God: "God, you have sent us here. My wife and I are the only missionaries in this area. God, how can we reach this multitude?"

God's answer to him was, "One at a time, Keith, one at a time." Keith rose from his knees and went out again to look for that one. He saw that a woman, jostled on the road, had dropped her load of merchandise. People were walking on her belongings, trampling the load under their feet. He went into the crowd and began to help her pull the materials together. He said to her: "Mother, you're hot and tired. Will you come into my yard and sit down and have something cool to drink?" He carried her load and led her to the yard.

She asked him, "Sir, why did you do that—get down in the dirt, help pick up my merchandise, and offer me this cool drink and a chance to rest?"

Keith responded, "I am so glad you asked me that," and he went on the tell her about Jesus. She accepted Christ as her Savior.

God's way is one at a time. God's time and place are whenever and wherever we have the opportunity.

3. *Discipleship* is an important purpose of the church. The Great Commission is more than a call to make converts. It is a call to make disciples (see Matt. 28:19-20). Disciples are pupils in the school of Jesus. They are learners and followers. Discipleship involves growth in knowledge and commitment. It also involves the discovery of spiritual gifts and a willingness to use those gifts in ministry.

A church develops disciples through Bible study, training opportunities, and involvement in ministry. Discipleship development is an ongoing process. Church Training, especially, focuses on this development. The goal is to develop mature, doctrinally sound, effective Christians who are able to serve Christ through the church.

4. *Fellowship* is an all-encompassing purpose of the church. The New Testament word for *fellowship, koinonia,* is used frequently in the New Testament in connection with believers. They had *koinonia* with one another, with Christ, and through the Spirit. The use of the word characterizes the church as a fellowship of believers, bound together by the Spirit, whose foundation is Jesus Christ.

Ken Lyle tells of an incident he heard about while living in New York City. A little girl had been playing in a fenced playground. When the time came for her to come in, she was nowhere to be found. Her mother and father began to look for her, and neighbors joined in the search. Finally, they called the police. After a long while, they heard her coming up the stairway. They had a parental urge to spank her and hug her at the same time. They asked anxiously, "Where have you been?"

She answered: "I have been helping Kathy. The head came off her doll, and I helped her try to put the head back on, but we couldn't get it on, so I have been helping Kathy cry."

We can't always solve people's problems, but when we cannot, at least we can be there to help them cry.

PERSONAL LEARNING ACTIVITY 9

When Jesus spoke of the church, He called it "my church." Christ's ownership of the church has many implications. Answer the questions below in light of that ownership.

1. What are the implications for the worship practices of the church?

_____

_____

_____

2. What are the implications for the activities of the church?

_____

_____

3. What are the implications for the priorities of the church?

_____

_____

1. Herschel H. Hobbs, *A Layman's Handbook of Christian Doctrine* (Nashville: Broadman Press, 1974), 32.
2. W. A. Criswell, *The Doctrine of the Church* (Nashville: Convention Press, 1980), 46-47.
3. Bill J. Leonard, *The Nature of the Church*, Layman's Library of Christian Doctrine (Nashville: Broadman Press, 1986), 46-47.
4. W. A. Criswell, *Criswell's Guidebook for Pastors* (Nashville: Broadman Press, 1980), 372.
5. Walter T. Conner, *The Gospel of Redemption* (Nashville: Broadman Press, 1945), 277.

CHAPTER 10

Last Things

*Then I saw a new heaven and a new earth, for the
first heaven and the first earth had passed away, and
there was no longer any sea. I saw the Holy City,
the new Jerusalem, coming down out of heaven from
God, prepared as a bride beautifully dressed for her
husband. And I heard a loud voice from the throne
saying, "Now the dwelling of God is with men, and
he will live with them. They will be his people, and
God himself will be with them and be their God. He
will wipe every tear from their eyes. There will be
no more death or mourning or crying or pain, for the
old order of things has passed away."*
Revelation 21:1-4

THE BIBLE PRESENTS HUMAN HIS-
tory as moving toward a divinely directed
goal. History is not cyclical, with events recurring in an eternal
cycle, nor is it evolutionary, progressing under its own power.
Rather, it is moving in a direction determined by God. It will
reach the goal that He has ordained.

LINEAR

Christians refer to the study of history's goal as eschatology,
the study of Last Things. This study of Christian doctrine will
conclude with a study of eschatology.

All Christians do not believe the same things in this vital doctrinal area. People who are equally sincere and devout often disagree about Last Things. Baptists have rightly refused to make
eschatology a test of orthodoxy and fellowship. But even though
various viewpoints about the future are held, all Christians believe that God is at work in history, that Jesus will return, and
that those who know Him will share in His glory. The goal toward which history is moving is beautifully expressed in Revelation 11:15: "'The kingdom of the world has become the

kingdom of our Lord and of his Christ, and he will reign for ever and ever.'"

Our study of Last Things will lead us to consider in brief fashion several important truths.

Last Things: Death and the Intermediate State

Death, rather than the second coming of Christ, is the time when most people will meet God face to face. Its reality often is ignored, but those who accept its certainty often reorder their lives.

Christians should think through the doctrine of death, for its meaning is quite different than for the unredeemed. Death for the Christian has been compared to birth. When the infant is in the process of being born into this earthly life, he resists. The womb is a comfortable environment and the only one he has known, and he does not want to leave it. The pain of birth causes him to resist. But when he enters the world outside the womb, he finds a much larger world, so large that he spends his life learning about it. Love and joy and a hundred other emotions enrich his existence.

When a Christian dies, he resists the experience, for it is painful, and the world beyond is unknown. The womb of this world is comfortable, and it is the world he knows. Yet when he passes through the womb of death, he is born into a new world that is much greater than earthly life—just as earthly life had proved to be greater than life in the mother's womb. Eternal life with the Master, with its absence of sin and sorrow, with love and joy and a thousand other experiences, enriches his existence.

Christians believe that the body will be resurrected (see 1 Cor. 15). The question that troubles many is, What happens to the Christian between the time of his death and the resurrection of his body at the end of time? At least two nonbiblical answers to this question are often heard. One of these ideas is often referred to as soul sleeping. Those who hold to this view believe that the soul is in an unconscious state between death and resurrection. Proponents of this belief point to such biblical passages as 1 Thessalonians 4:13, which refers to departed believers as "those who fall asleep." In such verses Herschel H. Hobbs points out that *sleep* is used "as a synonym for death as a cessation of labor, sorrow, and trouble."[1] The New Testament does not support belief in soul sleeping.

Another idea about the fate of the believer at the time of death is the doctrine of purgatory. Simply stated, this view teaches that purgatory is a place or condition in which those who die in a state of grace are purified and made ready to enter heaven. This intermediate state is for those who, although redeemed, are not yet free from imperfection. In purgatory they make expiation for unforgiven sins. This view is not a biblical doctrine, finding no support in either the Old or the New Testament.

Since these nonbiblical answers do not suffice, we must look further to answer, What happens to the Christian between the time of his death and the time of his final resurrection? In his book *The Life Beyond* Ray Summers states his preference for the term *disembodied* to refer to the time after death and before the resurrection of the body. The term more often used to describe this period is *intermediate state*. Summers feels that *disembodied* is better than *intermediate* because it is more descriptive and because it avoids some false interpretation. Obviously, when we die, our bodies are put aside, and we go back to the earth. Thus, we are "disembodied." Summers defines the disembodied state as *"the conscious existence of both the righteous and the wicked after death and prior to the resurrection."*[2]

The Christian spends this time in the presence of the Lord. The apostle Paul affirmed this truth to the Corinthians: "Therefore we are always confident and know that as long as we are at home in the body we are away from the Lord. We are confident, I say, and would prefer to be away from the body and at home with the Lord" (2 Cor. 5:6,8). When one who believes in Jesus Christ dies, that person is "at home" with the Lord. The body has been laid aside, and a new, resurrected body is promised; but in the meantime, the person is with the Lord.

When believers die and go to be with the Lord, they are said to be in paradise. Jesus promised the repentant thief that he would be with Him in paradise that day—the very day of the man's death (see Luke 23:43). The word *paradise* is used in two other

New Testament passages. In 2 Corinthians 12:4 Paul described an experience in which he said that he was "caught up to Paradise." Revelation 2:7 promises: "'To him who overcomes, I will give the right to eat from the tree of life, which is in the paradise of God.'"

The word *paradise*, generally agreed to be of Persian origin, refers to a beautiful garden or park, perhaps near the king's palace. As used in the Bible, *paradise* refers to the presence of God. When the righteous die, they go to be with God in paradise, a state of blessedness, rest, and joy.

Ray Summers summarizes the teachings of the Bible about the state of those who die trusting Jesus. First, theirs is a conscious state. They are alive and aware in the presence of God. Second, theirs is a fixed state. There is no biblical basis for a second chance after death, such as a purgatory for cleansing. The person's destiny has been determined by her reaction to God's offer of salvation. In the third place, the state of those who die trusting the Lord is an incomplete state. Since man is body as well as spirit, redemption will not be complete until the resurrection of the body.[3]

But what of those who die outside faith in Jesus Christ? What is their condition between the time of their death and their final judgment? When such people die, their bodies go back to the earth, but what of their spirits?

Baptists do not accept the nonbiblical idea of annihilation. This idea teaches that the souls of the wicked are annihilated, destroyed, and forever dead. The Bible, however, clearly teaches otherwise. In biblical thought, everyone who dies, righteous or wicked, goes into hades. The Greek word *hades* and the Hebrew equivalent word *sheol* mean *the realm of the dead.* Unfortunately, the King James Version translates these words as *hell*, but *hades* is the general term for the realm of the dead and does not necessarily refer to a place of punishment. There is a final hell for unbelievers, just as there is a final heaven for those who believe.

Luke 16:19-31 gives us the well-known story of the rich man and Lazarus. Both men died. Lazarus was carried to Abraham's side (see v. 22), where he was comforted (see v. 25). Obviously,

Lazarus was conscious in a state of rest, comfort, and joy. His condition was that of a saved person in paradise, although that word is not used in this passage.

The very opposite was true for the rich man. He went to hades; but for him, it was torment and agony. He was conscious of his suffering and cried out for just a drop of water to ease that suffering (see vv. 23-24). Even this prayer could not be answered. The barrier between his suffering and Lazarus's peace was insurmountable. Abraham responded to his request by saying: "'Between us and you a great chasm has been fixed, so that those who want to go from here to you cannot, nor can anyone cross over from there to us'" (Luke 16:26).

Peter assured his readers that "the Lord knows how to rescue godly men from trials and to hold the unrighteous for the day of judgment, while continuing their punishment" (2 Pet. 2:9). Of this passage Ray Summers writes, "This indicates that the unrighteous enter immediately into a state of punishment and that they experience that punishment until the time of final judgment."[4]

Although the suffering of the unrighteous during the disembodied state is not their final hell, it is clear that those who die outside Christ go to a place of punishment. Summers concludes his discussion of the punishment of the wicked between the time of death and the final judgment by making three important points. First, the state of the unrighteous after death is a conscious state. Second, the state of the unrighteous is a fixed state. Remember that the rich man in Luke 16 was clearly told that his situation could not be changed. Finally, the state of the unrighteous dead is an incomplete state. The resurrection, the final judgment, and hell are still ahead.[5]

The intermediate or disembodied state, then, is a time of conscious joy for the saved and conscious punishment for the lost. When we die, we experience one or the other.

Last Things: the Resurrection of the Body

John 5:25 records these words of Jesus: "'I tell you the truth, a time is coming and has now come when the dead will hear the voice of the Son of God and those who hear will live.'" A few verses later He is reported to have said, "'Do not be amazed at this, for a time is coming when all who are in their graves will hear his voice and come out—those who have done good will rise to live, and those who have done evil will rise to be condemned'" (John 5:28-29).

The resurrection of the body is clearly taught in the Bible. Even though those who have died are already either in paradise or in punishment, humans are not destined to spend eternity in a disembodied state. The resurrection awaits all of us.

References to the resurrection of the body are abundant in the New Testament. Paul emphasized in 1 Corinthians 15 the importance of the doctrine to Christian faith itself. Christ was raised from the dead, a fact witnessed by many (see 1 Cor. 15:3-8). His resurrection is the basis of the believer's hope to be raised from death (see vv. 20-22). If, on the other hand, there is no resurrection of the body, even Christ has not been raised, and our faith is hopeless and futile (see vv. 12-19).

Bodily resurrection means both the continuation of life and its fulfillment. Eternal life begins with the new birth. The believer starts a new existence in Christ but is bound to this world with its temptations and human frailties. Yet even as the Christian faces death with normal human dread, he looks beyond to a future life. Those who rightly understand the resurrection are able to face persecution even to death, for they know that death is no more than a painful experience and not the end. This knowledge provides us with a new dimension of life. We march to a different drummer; we can resist the pressures of the world to force us into its mold; we can think thoughts and take actions on the basis of God's eternal economy rather than that of the world.

The form of the resurrected body troubled the Corinthians, and it troubles some believers today. If the body decays and is recycled in nature, how can it be raised? Paul's answer is that bodily resurrection does not mean that we will have the same flesh-and-blood body that we now have (see vv. 35-44). The natural body is not to be compared to the resurrection body. Somehow, God will shape for each person a body suited to the resurrection. The form of the body is not important; what is important is that we will not be disembodied spirits or absorbed into some ethereal idea. We will be real persons, with real identities and real personalities. The body God provides will not be subject to aging, decay, and death (see 1 Cor. 15:53-54; Rev. 21:4).

We are informed about the nature of this resurrection body by the nature of Jesus' body after He arose from the dead. John said that we would be like Him (1 John 3:2). He had a body, and it was one in which the disciples recognized Him (see Luke 24:36-43; John 20:19-20,24-29). Jesus' body, however, was not subject to earthly laws. He was able to disappear while they were looking (see Luke 24:31) and appear to the disciples in spite of locked doors (see John 20:19). Yet they could touch Him (see John 20:27) and even eat with Him (see John 21:10-14).

When will the resurrection of the body take place? Paul addresses this question in 1 Corinthians 15:51-52: "Listen, I tell you a mystery: We will not all sleep, but we will all be changed—in a flash, in the twinkling of an eye, at the last trumpet. For the trumpet will sound, the dead will be raised imperishable, and we will be changed." The idea of the trumpet relates to the return of Jesus. When the believers who have died are resurrected and those who are alive when Jesus returns are transformed, all of God's people will have imperishable and immortal bodies. Death will be forever defeated. Victory will belong to God's people (see 1 Cor. 15:53-56).

The unrighteous will also be resurrected. Many texts in the Bible affirm this truth. Some of these passages are: Daniel 12:2; Acts 24:15; Revelation 20:12-13; and John 5:18-29. When will the resurrection of the unrighteous take place? Many Christians believe that one general resurrection of the righteous and the unrighteous will occur at the second coming of Christ. Other Christians understand the Bible to teach two resurrections. These believe that the righteous will be resurrected when Jesus returns for His church and that the unrighteous will be resurrected following a thousand-year reign of Christ on earth. This reign is referred to as the millennium. Those who hold to this view find support in such passages as Revelation 20:4-6 and 1 Thessalonians 4:13-18.

Last Things: Christ's Second Coming

Southern Baptists have never made views of the second coming a test of faith apart from the conviction that Christ will literally return and establish a new heaven and earth. All of the primary views held throughout Christian history are held by various Southern Baptists.

The views are referred to as millennial in reference to what one believes about the millennium. The word *millennium* does not appear in the Bible. A Latin word meaning *thousand,* it refers to the thousand-year reign of Christ suggested in Revelation 20:2-7. Adding *pre* to the word (premillennial) indicates a belief that Christ will return prior to the millennium; adding *post* (postmillennial) indicates a belief that Christ will return after the millennium; adding *a* (amillennial—*a* means *no*) refers to a belief that the millennium is not a literal reign but refers to the time extending from Jesus' ascension to His second coming. The premillennial view is further divided into two primary views, similar in some respects and quite different in others.

Postmillennialists are rare today, but the view was very strong during the late nineteenth century and up until World War I. The interpretation holds that through aggressive evangelism and missions the world will be won to Christ. Jesus will come to reign in believers' hearts—and thus in the world—so thoroughly that a thousand-year reign of Christ on earth will be ushered in. At the end of the thousand years Satan will attempt once again to rally his forces and attack God, but he will be defeated, and Christ will inaugurate a new heaven and earth. B. H. Carroll, founder of Southwestern Baptist Theological Seminary, was a leading proponent of the view.

Amillennialists interpret Revelation and other prophetic passages symbolically. The millennium is not a literal reign but rather represents the reign of God in the hearts of believers. It is very wrong to accuse those who hold to this view of not believing in the literal return of Christ, for they definitely do. In fact, this view sets no events or conditions that must take place before Christ returns. Thus, it allows for the coming of Christ at any time. The view was introduced by Augustine in the fourth century and was the dominant one among Christians for a thousand years until the Reformation. It is a popular view among many Southern Baptists. Well-known advocates of this position are Ray Summers and Herschel Hobbs.

Historical premillennialists interpret Revelation and other texts much as did the Christian world from the New Testament period up to Augustine. This view holds that God's people will grow in strength, but Satan's power also will become more evident. In the end of time a literal Antichrist will arise and deceive the world; many will follow him, resulting in terrible persecution of those who remain faithful. God will use the Jews once again in a way the Bible does not reveal, but they will be saved by grace through faith just as Gentiles are. A literal seven-year period of great tribulation will begin, through which the church will suffer. At the end of that time Christ will return, and believers will rise to meet Him in the air. He will defeat Satan in a literal battle of Armageddon and establish a literal thousand-year reign. At the end of that time Satan will gather his forces for one last assault on God and will be defeated. Then come the judgment and the establishing of the new heaven and earth. Many who hold this view feel that the numbers in Revelation may be symbolic and are not to be forced to indicate literal lengths of time (seven, one thousand, etc.), but all believe in the literalness of the prophesied events.

Dispensational premillennialists believe that history is divided into dispensations in which God works through different methods. Dispensations include pre-Israel, Israel, the church age, and the millennial kingdom, among others. Writers differ on some details, but essentially this interpretation agrees with the historical premillennial position on the rise of the Antichrist, the great tribulation period, the battle of Armageddon, the thousand-year reign, the battle at the end of the reign, the judgment, and the new heaven and earth. However, within those agreements a quite different approach to prophecy results in quite different conclusions. For example, many believe that Revelation 2 and 3 are not only letters to churches. Instead, each church represents a distinct church age, and we currently are in the last one, the age of apostasy. The nation of Israel will be reestablished, for it is still God's Chosen People. Christ will return part way to earth, at

Church Covenant   +   +

...g been led, as we believe by the Spirit of God, to receive ... Lord Jesus Christ as our Savior and, on the profession of our faith, having been baptized in the name of the Father, and of the Son, and of the Holy Spirit, we do now, in the presence of God, and this assembly, most solemnly and joyfully enter into covenant with one another as one body in Christ.

We engage, therefore, by the aid of the Holy Spirit to walk together in Christian love; to strive for the advancement of this church, in knowledge, holiness, and comfort; to promote its prosperity and spirituality; to sustain its worship, ordinances, discipline, and doctrines; to contribute cheerfully and regularly to the support of the ministry, the expenses of the church, the relief of the poor, and the spread of the gospel through all nations.

We also engage to maintain family and secret devotions; to religiously educate our children; to seek the salvation of our kindred and acquaintances; to walk circumspectly in the world; to be just in our dealings, faithful in our engagements, and exemplary in our deportment; to avoid all tattling, back-biting, and excessive anger; to abstain from the sale of, and use of, destructive drugs or intoxicating drinks as a beverage; to shun pornography; to be zealous in our efforts to advance the Kingdom of our Savior.

We further engage to watch over one another in brotherly love; to remember one another in prayer; to aid one another in sickness and distress; to cultivate Christian sympathy in feeling and Christian courtesy in speech; to be slow to take offense, but always ready for reconciliation and mindful of the rules of our Savior to secure it without delay.

We moreover engage that when we remove from this place we will, as soon as possible, unite with some other church where we can carry out the spirit of this covenant and the principles of God's Word.

CODE 4361-02   BROADMAN & HOLMAN PUBLISHERS

which time the true church will be raptured to meet Christ in the air. This is the beginning of the great tribulation. Christians will not go through this tribulation. During that time, they will be judged and will be receiving assignments for the coming millennial kingdom. During the first half of the great tribulation the Antichrist will deceive the Jews into supporting him. Then the Jews will realize their error and turn to God. This will result in severe persecution of the Jews. Nevertheless, many will be won to Christ by joining the kingdom. Christ will return at the end of the great tribulation and establish the millennium, during which He will rule the world with a rod of iron from Jerusalem, working through those who have been appointed to various positions of authority earlier. The events at the end of the millennium are similar to those described by historical premillennialists, except that dispensationalists hold to several resurrections and several judgments. This view arose during the nineteenth century among Plymouth Brethren in England and became popular in the United States through widespread Bible conferences and the publication of the Scofield Reference Bible. Many Southern Baptists hold to this view.

Whichever view one holds, it is essential for biblical faith that one believe in the literal return of Christ. *The Baptist Faith and Message* is intentionally vague on the manner of Christ's return but is forceful on the fact of it.

The certainty of Christ's return is based solidly on Scripture (see John 14:28; Acts 1:10-11; 1 Thess. 4:16). It has provided Christians with reassurance during times of persecution, but that is not the only reason to study the subject. A mature understanding of this doctrine provides enormous power to the Christian to be aggressive in evangelism, missions, and ethics. Disagreements about interpretation should not keep Christians from studying this important part of God's revelation to us.

Last Things: Judgment and Eternal Destiny

The end time will be a time of judgment, after God has sought again and again to bring people to redemption. God as judge was discussed in chapter 2, but the point must be reinforced that eternal judgment is sure (Rev. 20:12-13). No one will escape it, whether believer or nonbeliever. The Christian is safe in the blood of Christ, but even so both joy and sorrow will abound when each of us stands before God's judgment and answers for our faithfulness (Rom. 14:10-12; 2 Cor. 5:10). The feeble excuses we give for not putting God first that seem so understandable to us today will stand in stark contrast to what God reveals as truly important. The unredeemed will quake before God as He states with amazing detail the number of times they had opportunities to repent and did not, and their sentences of condemnation will be seen to be righteous.

The Bible does not tell us a great deal about heaven, but it nevertheless affirms the reality of heaven and describes it in terms that picture incredible glory. Several truths found in the Bible about heaven are: (1) it is a place (see John 14:2); (2) Jesus will be there (see John 14:3); (3) God will be there (see Rev. 21:22-23); (4) no sin or suffering but only purity will be there (see Rev. 21:4,27; 22:1-3); (5) different levels of reward will be assigned, based on faithfulness (see Matt. 25:14-30); (6) we will know and understand (see 1 Cor. 13:8-12); (7) we will praise God constantly with great joy (see Rev. 5:11-13; 15:2-4).

The Bible deals also with the reality of hell. One Hebrew word and three Greek words are translated *hell* in the King James Version. The Hebrew *sheol* and the Greek *hades* and *tartarsas* refer to death in general or the general realm of the dead. In the New Testament the teaching is clearer. There the Greek *gehenna* refers to the place of condemnation for the unredeemed. Recent translations of the Bible help us see these differences. *Gehenna*, rightly translated *hell*, was the garbage dump in the Hinnom valley just south of Jerusalem that burned continually. It was a cursed place because it was used for pagan human sacrifice during the days of the monarchy (see 2 Chron. 28:1-3; 33:1-6). After Josiah's reforms the place was used for the city dump, including the disposal of dead animals and the bodies of executed criminals. Thus, the word indicates curse as well as continual burning. The Bible's use of this word to describe hell should settle any debate about the existence of a place of eternal torment. Its existence is quite clear, regardless of how people debate it.

Jesus referred to hell in this sense several times (see Matt.

5:22,29-30; 18:9; 23:15; Mark 9:43-47; Luke 12:5). Revelation describes hell as a lake of fire (20:14-15). Jesus spoke of hell as a place where "'"their worm does not die, and the fire is not quenched"'" (Mark 9:48). Since all kinds of refuse were piled on the garbage dump outside the city (Gehenna), the maggots continually fed and multiplied. The fire never went out. It blazed or smoldered continually. The words "not quenched" come from the Greek word *asbeston,* from which we get the English word *asbestos.* It means something that can be placed in fire but will never burn up. So Jesus' statement depicts the idea of ongoing punishment. Other words of Jesus concerning hell are found in Matthew 10:28; 13:41-42,49-50; 23:33; 25:41,46; Luke 16:22-23; John 5:28-29. John in Revelation calls hell "the lake of fire" (Rev. 20:15); in Revelation 19:20, "the fiery lake of burning sulfur." When all these New Testament references are put together, a terrible picture emerges of a place of burning that never ceases, a lake of fire.

It is logical to believe in hell if we believe in a hereafter. If there is a land of joy and rest for God's faithful people, there is a hell for the unredeemed. In the Scripture this is made abundantly clear. Daniel 12:2 says, "'Multitudes who sleep in the dust of the earth will awake: some to everlasting life, others to shame and everlasting contempt.'" The foundational principle of justice demands a heaven and a hell. In this world those who live outside the laws of society are considered dangerous and disruptive and are put in prison or segregated from the law-abiding citizens. This separation is necessary for the good of society and to protect the innocent. Logical justice demands that there is a hell. People who live outside the will and mercy of God are rebellious people who are unfit for the righteousness and purity of heaven. The Bible teaches that sin destroys people's lives and sends them to hell. It is not a matter of how much God loves people; it is the rejection of that love that condemns.

Last Things: a New Heaven and Earth
The consumation of history will take place when the world as it is passes away and a new heaven and earth are created (Rev. 21:1). We do not know all that event means either for the creation or for

us personally, but we have glimpses of its glory. We are to wait for it expectantly (2 Pet. 3:13). Paul wrote of its coming in exalted terms: of creation being set free, of groaning in the pain of child-birth until that time of redemption (Rom. 8:18-22).

Paul described that coming event in 1 Corinthians 15:24-28. Every enemy will be defeated, even death, and then Christ will deliver the kingdom to His Father. This subject cannot be sepa-rated from Christ's work of redemption, for it is the ultimate development of the kingdom of Christ, the reign of Christ in the hearts of people. Walter T. Conner wrote, "It is not to be some-thing unrelated to, or out of line with, what he did in founding that kingdom."[6] His second coming, as Conner also pointed out, does not mean that Jesus left this world not to be active again in it until He returns; rather, He rules even now from heaven's throne, working to move history toward the great consummation of the age.[7] The perfect society that we learn about in the Sermon on the Mount and other teachings of Jesus and that we are com-manded to work for now will be realized, for only the redeemed will be there, and God will be its light.

As a seventeen-year-old boy, I sat with my mother as she died. She spoke, but I did not understand and asked her what she was saying. She spoke again and said, "I see Jesus." She lifted her hand as to greet someone and then died with a peaceful and joyous expression on her face. Jesus promises, "'If I go and pre-pare a place for you, I will come back and take you to be with me that you also may be where I am'" (John 14:3).

As Christians we can be certain that God is in control and holds the future in His hands. Whether we go to meet Him through death or live to see His triumphant coming, we, too, are in His hands.

PERSONAL LEARNING ACTIVITY 10

Christians hold several viewpoints on the second coming of Christ. Four views are discussed in this chapter. Briefly define each view listed below. Look back to pages 133-135 if you need to refresh your memory.

Then circle the one that most nearly represents your view of the second coming.

Postmillennialism: _____

_____

Amillennialism: _____

_____

Historical premillennialism: _____

_____

Dispensational premillennialism: _____

_____

_____

1. Herschel H. Hobbs, *A Layman's Handbook of Christian Doctrine* (Nashville: Broadman Press, 1974), 51.
2. Ray Summers, *The Life Beyond* (Nashville: Broadman Press, 1959), 18-19.
3. Ibid., 23-24.
4. Ibid., 25.
5. Ibid., 29.
6. Walter T. Conner, *The Gospel of Redemption* (Nashville: Broadman Press, 1945), 326-327.
7. Ibid., 331.

Teaching Guide

Introduction

THIS TEACHING GUIDE CONTAINS DETAILED TEACH-
ing plans to assist you in leading a group study of *The Doctrines
Baptists Believe*. The plans can be used with either a large or a
small group.

The teaching plans in this guide are self-contained—that is,
they enable you to lead good sessions without additional resources. However, the plans frequently suggest the use of teaching posters, agree/disagree statements, and other learning aids.
These tools enrich the sessions and involve group members actively in the learning process.

Learning Goals

Upon completion of this course, each group member should have
a better understanding of a number of the doctrines Baptists believe and their implications for his or her life. Each session has a
specific learning goal related to this general goal. The learning
goals will help you to maintain a focus as you lead the sessions.

Planning Actions

1. Nothing can substitute for study and prayer. Pray for the
guidance of the Holy Spirit as you prepare for and lead the sessions.
2. Encourage the participants to read the appropriate chapters in
The Doctrines Baptists Believe in preparation for each session.
3. Prepare a poster outline of the session titles to use in all of the
sessions. Prepare a 1 by 4 arrow pointer from poster board and
glue the arrow to a clothespin. Use this pointer with the outline
poster.

THE DOCTRINES BAPTISTS BELIEVE

Session 1: The Bible: the Inspired Word of God
The Doctrine of God
(Chapters 1 and 2)
Session 2: In God's Image
The Doctrine of Christ
(Chapters 3 and 4)
Session 3: The Atoning Work of Christ
The Doctrine of Salvation
(Chapters 5 and 6)
Session 4: The Christian Life: Priests of God
The Christian Life: Living in the Spirit
(Chapters 7 and 8)
Session 5: The Church
Last Things
(Chapters 9 and 10)

4. If you have a large number of person in the study, small-group work can be handled easily. Simply divide into as many small groups as necessary to involve everyone. The same assignment can be given to more than one small group. For example, if the teaching plan calls for five small groups to be given five assignments and one hundred persons are in the study, form twenty-five small groups. Five groups would be given the first assignment, five groups the second assignment, and so on.

5. Make extensive use of the Bible as you teach. It is the textbook for studying the doctrines Baptists believe. The Bible alone is our authority for faith and practice.

6. Use your imagination in preparing for and leading the sessions. Do not feel bound by the suggestions in this guide.

7. Begin and close each session with prayer.

8. Following each session, spend some time evaluating the session. Think of ways you can improve future sessions.

9. The following hymn was written especially for this doctrine study. A stanza is devoted to each of the ten chapters in the book. You may want your group to sing the appropriate stanza as you teach each chapter.

THE DOCTRINES BAPTISTS BELIEVE

William H. Stephens

Sing to the tune of the hymn "Lord, Send a Revival."

1. God's Holy Word, what a joy to read;
   His direct voice, it's my only creed.
   Witness to Jesus, inspired, each word;
   Deeply my soul is stirred.
   O witnessing, truthful Word;
   O pow'rful, compelling Word;
   O gift of revealing God;
   By Holy Spirit heard.

2. Sov'reign Creator, Almighty God;
   Mountains and valleys Your foot has trod.
   Awesome and holy we hold Your name;
   Yet to our midst You came!
   O e'er-present, caring Lord;
   O all-knowing, loving Lord;
   O all-pow'rful, saving Lord;
   I raise to You this hymn.

3. Favored of God, man creation's goal;
   Image of Him: spirit, mind, and soul.
   Once walked with God, sinful, fallen race;
   Blind, depraved, and base.
   O thinking yet scheming ones;
   O free yet rebellious ones;
   O strong yet weakly ones;
   You are in need of grace.

4. Jesus is Prophet, and Priest, and King;
   He is the Ruler of everything.
   Savior, Redeemer, and Lord is He;
   He lived and died for me.
   O human and hurting One;
   O God and eternal One;
   O Christ of the Three in One;
   I give my all to Thee!

5. Emptied Himself, Jesus Christ came down;
   Dwelt among men, gave up heav'n and crown.
   Suffering Servant, He showed His way;
   Then died my price to pay.
   O healing, redeeming Lord;
   O crucified, suff'ring Lord;
   O glorified, risen Lord;
   You conquered death for me!

6. How to be saved people long have sought;
   Turning to Christ, what fierce wars are fought!
   You must repent of your life and will;
   Then confess Christ and yield.
   O what a great joy is He!
   O what purpose, now I'm free!
   O hope clearly now I see!
   Thy presence my life fill.

7. I am a priest by redemption's price;
   No one between God and me save Christ!
   High Priest, He rent the veil in twain,
   New cov'nant bought in pain!
   O ev'ry believer's right!
   O truth of the churches' might;
   O access to Abba's light!
   Lord, we sing this refrain.

8. Minist'ring, serving mankind each day;
   Ev'ry believer must show the way,
   Led by God's Spirit to lost mankind,
   Each dark recess to find.
   O holiness is Your call!
   O ministry is Your call!
   O witnessing is Your call!
   We are called soul and mind.

9. Body of Christ, in you He does dwell;
   Ne'er to succumb to the gates of hell;
   Sinners redeemed held by Christ's strong hand;
   Such is this might band!
   O family of Christ on earth!
   O col'ny of heav'n on earth!

O Bride when He comes to earth!
In You we seek to stand.

10. One day I'll cross o'er the stormy sea;
On that far shore Jesus waits for me.
Death, through your womb to eternal life,
End to this world of strife!
O death now where is your sting?
O joyf'lly for heav'n I sing!
O to Jesus' breast I cling!
By His great light I see.

Session 1

The Bible: the Inspired Word of God
The Doctrine of God
(Chapters 1 and 2)

Learning goal: After completing this session, participants should have a better understanding of the doctrines of the Bible and of God. They will be able to: (1) explain in their own words at least four basic beliefs about the Bible and (2) explain in their own words at least four basic beliefs about God.

Before the Session

1. Have copies of *The Doctrines Baptists Believe* available for participants. Have registration materials and a Baptist Doctrine Diploma available.

2. Prepare a copy of the following true/false pretest for each member. (1) The Bible is inspired in the same sense that other great books or poems are inspired. (2) Some parts of the Bible are more inspired than other parts. (3) God is one and has made Himself known as three Persons. (4) Pantheism is the view that God is everywhere at all times. (5) Persons have the freedom to choose between right and wrong. (6) Sin basically is ignorance of the will of God. (7) Jesus Christ is fully divine and also fully human. (8) Jesus rejected the term *Lord* for Himself. (9) The main work of Jesus on earth was to be our example. (10) *Predestination* means that God has predetermined that some persons will be saved and others will be lost. (11) The term *atonement* refers to the reconciling act of God by which He dealt once for all with the sin that separates persons from God. (12) *Regeneration* means *the unmerited favor of God.* (13) All believers have equality before God. (14) Sanctification is a once-for-all act whereby God declares the sinner justified. (15) Every believer receives the Holy Spirit at the time of conversion. (16) To be filled with the Spirit means to be controlled by the Spirit. (17) The word *church* in the New Testament always refers to a local body of believers. (18) Baptism and the Lord's Supper are sacraments through which the

church dispenses grace. (19) The resurrection of the body is not taught in Scripture. (20) All judgment is here in this life.

3. Prepare the following agree/disagree statements. You can write the statements on the chalkboard; you can write them on strips of adding-machine tape and attach the strips to the board or wall; or you can make copies to hand out. (1) Those who insist on the absolute truthfulness and authority of the written Word of God tend to worship the Bible rather than the God who gave it. (2) No person knows exactly how God inspired the writing of Scripture. (3) The criterion by which we interpret the Bible is the church. (4) Creeds have been a valid place in Baptist life. (5) The term *Trinity* refers to the succession of ways God has appeared in history. (6) There has never been a time when God did not exist. (7) God has revealed enough of Himself through nature for a person to be saved. (8) The Bible does not reveal why God created the universe.

4. Write the following statements on large sheets of newsprint. "All Scripture is God-breathed" (2 Tim. 3:16). "The word of our God shall stand for ever" (Isa. 40:8, KJV). The Bible is divine in its origin. When we believe the Word of God, we believe God. The Bible is truth, without any mixture of error. The Bible is a beacon to show wanderers the way to go. The eternal God reveals Himself to us as Father, Son, and Holy Spirit. Wherever we are, at any time, God is there. God has "measured the waters in the hollow of his hand" (Isa. 40:12). Our Heavenly Father reigns with providential care over His universe. Mount these teaching posters in random order on the walls around the room.

5. Place a small table at the front of the room. Place an open Bible in the center of the table. Also place the following objects on the table: a lamp, a hammer, a jar of honey, a sword or a knife, a loaf of bread, a glass of water, a mirror, and some seeds. Read the following Bible verses related to each symbol: lamp (Ps. 119:105); hammer (Jer. 23:29); honey (Ps. 119:103); sword (Eph. 6:17); bread (Matt. 4:4); water (Eph. 5:26); mirror (Jas. 1:23–25); seed (Luke 8:11).

6. Write the following words on strips of adding-machine tape: One, Spirit, Person, Infinite, Perfect, Creator, and Sovereign.

7. Prepare to speak on chapters 1 and 2, following the outline in the book. However, do *not* plan to lecture nonstop during the session. Plan to make the study a teaching/discussion session.

During the Session

1. Quickly care for administrative matters. Distribute copies of *The Doctrines Baptists Believe*. Show the Baptist Doctrine Diploma and explain how the diploma is earned. Encourage everyone to earn one.

2. Use the outline poster to overview the entire study. Share the general learning goal for the study. Emphasize the importance of doctrine and the need for each person to be well-grounded in the basic doctrines of our faith. Then focus on the topics for session 1.

3. Ask volunteers to read aloud the agree/disagree statements. As each statement is read, determine those who agree with the statement, those who disagree, and those who are undecided. If the group is divided in opinion, allow time for discussion of the statement.

4. Lecture on the points in chapter 1. Write the points on the chalkboard as you deal with each one. Allow time for discussion.

5. Call attention to the objects on the table. Ask members to share any Scripture passage that relates each object to the Word of God. Discuss the meaning of each symbol as it relates to the Bible.

6. Lecture and lead a discussion on the points in chapter 2. Mount each word strip (step 6, "Before the Session") to the chalkboard or wall as you discuss it.

7. Call attention to the teaching posters on the walls. Ask volunteers to read the statements and to comment on their meanings.

8. Distribute the pretest and ask members to complete it before the next session by marking the statements *T* (true) or *F* (false). (Answers are in session 5.)

Session 2

In God's Image
The Doctrine of Christ
(Chapters 3 and 4)

Learning goal: After completing this session, members should have a better understanding of the doctrine of man and the doctrine of Christ. They will be able to: (1) explain in their own words at least four basic beliefs about the doctrine of man and (2) explain in their own words at least four basic truths about Christ.

Before the Session
1. Write the following outline of chapter 4 on strips of adding-machine tape: (1) The Incarnation of God; (2) Born of a Virgin; (3) The Supreme Revelation; (4) Prophet, Priest, and King; (5) Divine and Human; (6) The Promised Messiah; (7) The High Priest; and (8) Lord and King.
2. Plan to lecture on and lead a discussion of chapter 4. Follow the outline in the book.
3. Prepare the following teaching posters. Mount them in random order on the walls. We are made in the image of God. Persons are the crown of God's creation. "All we like sheep have gone astray" (Isa. 53:6, KJV). Sin is rebellion against God. One of the greatest wastes of all is the waste of human potentiality (see Rom. 3:23). Jesus Christ is God. Jesus is greater than anything we can say about Him. Jesus Christ is too big for any definition. "He that hath seen me hath seen the Father" (John 14:9, KJV). "Jesus loves me! This I know."

During the Session
1. Call attention to the outline poster. Focus on session 2. Use personal learning activity (PLA) 3 as a basis for discussion to create interest in chapter 3.
2. Divide members into five small groups. Assign each group one of the following points from chapter 3: "In God's Image: Man, the Goal of Creation," "In God's Image: Persons Are Cre-

ated Free," "Fallen in Sin: the Origin and Nature of Sin," "Fallen in Sin: a Description of Sin," and "Fallen in Sin: the Results of Sin." Ask each group to summarize and explain its assigned topic. Allow time for group work and call for reports.
3. Lecture on and lead a discussion of chapter 4. Mount each word strip (step 1, "Before the Session") to the chalkboard or wall as you lecture.
4. Refer to PLA 4. Lead a discussion based on this activity.
5. Ask volunteers to read the teaching posters and to comment on their meanings.

Session 3

The Atoning Work of Christ
The Doctrine of Salvation
(Chapters 5 and 6)

Learning goal: After completing this session, members should have a better understanding of the atonement and the doctrine of salvation. They will be able to: (1) explain at least four biblical terms related to Christ's atonement; (2) explain the steps involved in salvation; and (3) explain what salvation means to the believer.

Before the Session
1. Plan to lecture on and lead a discussion of chapter 6.
2. Prepare the following agree/disagree statements. (1) Repentance involves a change of mind that allows God to change one's heart and life. (2) A person can receive Christ as Savior without accepting Him as Lord. (3) Saving faith does not involve the intellect. (4) The doctrine of the eternal security of the believer means that anyone who joins a church is secure. (5) Jesus did not die as a substitute for us. (6) *Redemption* refers to the deliverance from the bondage and consequences of sin. (7) *Reconciliation* means *reformation*. (8) The New Testament concept of justice and righteousness is based on keeping the law.
3. Prepare the following teaching posters. Mount them in random order on the walls. The cross is at the very center of the Christian faith. He who knew no sin became the sin bearer for humanity. "God so loved" (John 3:16). We are redeemed "with the precious blood of Christ" (1 Pet. 1:19). Christ died in our place. "Ye must be born again" (John 3:7, KJV). Faith is trust and obedience. *Forsaking All, I Trust Him.* Salvation is three-fold. Open confession of Christ speaks to the very nature of faith.

During the Session
1. Refer to the outline poster. Focus on session 3. Use the agree/disagree statements as a basis for discussion.

2. Divide members into four small groups. Assign each group one of the following sets of words: (1) *substitution/covenant;* (2) *sacrifice/redemption;* (3) *reconciliation/justification;* and (4) *propitiation/expiation.* Ask each group to study chapter 5 and to define each of the two assigned terms. Allow time for group work and call for reports.

3. Lecture on the doctrine of salvation, using the outline in the book. Allow time for discussion of the various points.

4. Refer to PLA 6. Call for volunteers to share their testimony, using the three-point outline.

5. Ask volunteers to read the teaching posters and to comment on their meanings.

Session 4

The Christian Life: Priests of God
The Christian Life: Living in the Spirit
(Chapters 7 and 8)

Learning goal: After completing this session, members should have a better understanding of the Christian life. They will be able to: (1) state three main truths about the doctrine of the priesthood of believers; (2) describe sanctification; and (3) describe the work of the Holy Spirit.

Before the Session
1. Prepare to lecture on and lead a discussion of chapters 7 and 8.
2. Prepare the following agree/disagree statements. (1) Some believers are called into ministry. (2) All believers are priests. (3) The word *sanctification* means *without sin.* (4) It is possible for a Christian to miss God's will for his or her life. (5) The Holy Spirit is a power or influence radiating from God. (6) The Holy Spirit deals only with Christians. (7) The gifts of the Spirit are the same as the fruit of the Spirit. (8) Every Christian has the fruit of the Spirit.
3. Prepare the following teaching posters. Mount them in random order on the walls. All believers are called by God to ministry. Each of us is a bridge builder. You and I are God's *naos.* Sanctification has three aspects. "I press toward the mark" (Phil. 3:14, KJV). "Grow in the grace and knowledge of our Lord and Savior Jesus Christ" (2 Pet. 3:18). Every believer receives the Holy Spirit at the time of conversion. The Holy Spirit provides the power for the Christian life. Life in the power of the Spirit is a life of discipleship. All of God's people are gifted.

During the Session
1. Refer to the outline poster and focus on session 4. Use the agree/disagree statements as the basis for discussion.

2. Lecture briefly on chapter 7, following the outline in the book. Allow time for discussion.

3. Refer to PLA 7 and ask volunteers to respond.

4. Lecture briefly on chapter 8 and allow time for discussion. Use the chalkboard to list the work of the Holy Spirit.

5. Refer to PLA 8 and ask members to respond.

6. Ask volunteers to read the teaching posters and to comment on their meanings.

Session 5

The Church
Last Things
(Chapters 9 and 10)

Learning goal: After completing this session, members should have a better understanding of the doctrines of the church and Last Things. They will be able to: (1) summarize in their own words at least two basic beliefs about the church; (2) explain in their own words the significance of baptism and the Lord's Supper; and (3) explain in their own words at least three biblical truths about Last Things.

Before the Session

1. Prepare to lecture on and lead a discussion of chapters 9 and 10.

2. Prepare copies of the true/false test used in session 1 to use as a posttest.

3. Prepare the following agree/disagree statements. (1) Simon Peter is the rock on which Christ built the church. (2) All believers of all the ages are part of the universal church. (3) Baptism is essential to salvation. (4) Baptism and the Lord's Supper are local church ordinances. (5) Belief about Last Things is a test of orthodoxy and fellowship in a Baptist church. (6) Eternal life for the believer begins with the second coming of Christ. (7) Only the righteous will be resurrected. (8) All judgment is finished for the believer.

4. Prepare the following teaching posters. Mount them in random order on the walls. "'On this rock I will build my church'" (Matt. 16:18). We must never forget that the church belongs to Jesus. The church is a community of believers. We are part of the family of God. History is His story. Death is the time when most people will meet God face to face. A person's destiny is determined by his or her response to Jesus Christ. Those who die without Christ go to a place of punishment. "I will come again"

(John 14:3, KJV). Heaven is a prepared place for a prepared people.

During the Session

1. Refer to the outline poster and briefly review the entire study. Then focus on session 5. Use the agree/disagree statements as the basis for discussion.

2. Lecture briefly on chapter 9, following the outline in the book. Allow time for discussion.

3. Refer to PLA 9 and ask members to respond.

4. Lecture briefly on chapter 10, following the outline in the book. Allow time for discussion.

5. Refer to PLA 10 and lead the group to summarize these four views.

6. Ask volunteers to read the teaching posters and to comment on their meanings.

7. Hand out the posttest and allow time for members to complete it. Discuss the answers. Answers: 1. *F;* 2. *F;* 3. *T;* 4. *F;* 5. *T;* 6. *F;* 7. *T;* 8. *F;* 9. *F;* 10. *F;* 11. *T;* 12. *F;* 13. *T;* 14. *F;* 15. *T;* 16. *T;* 17. *F;* 18. *F;* 19. *F;* 20. *F.*

8. Express appreciation to members for their participation in the study. Close by singing a hymn.

For more distinctives of Southern Baptist faith, check out a classic resource, newly revised

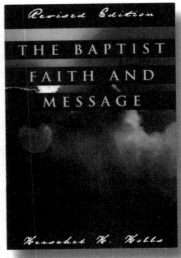

THE BAPTIST FAITH AND MESSAGE
by Herschel H. Hobbs

The revision of the 1971 edition is dedicated to Herschel H. Hobbs, author of *The Baptist Faith and Message*. It includes not only the articles of our faith, but new information Dr. Hobbs wrote just prior to his death.

This revised edition presents Baptists' basic beliefs about such things as Scriptures, God, salvation, grace, the church, the kingdom, evangelism, missions, education, stewardship, and more. *The Baptist Faith and Message* is an indispensible reference for all Southern Baptists! (ISBN 0-8054-9597-5)

To obtain more information or to place an order, contact Customer Service Center, MSN 113; 127 Ninth Avenue, North; Nashville, TN 37234-0113; Phone (800) 458-2772; Fax (615) 251-5933; Email customerservice@bssb.com.

CHRISTIAN GROWTH STUDY PLAN

Preparing Christians to Serve

In the **Christian Growth Study Plan (formerly Church Study Course),** this book **The Doctrines Baptists Believe** is a resource for course credit in the subject area **Baptist Doctrine** of the Christian Growth category of diploma plans. To receive credit, read the book, complete the learning activities, show your work to your pastor, a staff member or church leader, then complete the information on the next page. The form may be duplicated. Send the completed page to:

Christian Growth Study Plan
127 Ninth Avenue, North, MSN 117
Nashville, TN 37234-0117
FAX: (615)251-5067

For information about the Christian Growth Study Plan, refer to the current Christian Growth Study Plan Catalog. Your church office may have a copy. If not, request a free copy from the Christian Growth Study Plan office (615/251-2525).

The Doctrines Baptists Believe
COURSE NUMBER: CG-0148

PARTICIPANT INFORMATION

Social Security Number (USA ONLY)	Personal CGSP Number*	Date of Birth (MONTH, DAY, YEAR)
- -	-	- -

Name (First, Middle, Last)		Home Phone
☐ Mr. ☐ Miss		-
☐ Mrs.		

Address (Street, Route, or P.O. Box)	City, State, or Province	Zip/Postal Code

CHURCH INFORMATION

Church Name

Address (Street, Route, or P.O. Box)	City, State, or Province	Zip/Postal Code

CHANGE REQUEST ONLY

☐ Former Name

☐ Former Address	City, State, or Province	Zip/Postal Code

☐ Former Church	City, State, or Province	Zip/Postal Code

Signature of Pastor, Conference Leader, or Other Church Leader	Date

*New participants are requested but not required to give SS# and date of birth. Existing participants, please give CGSP# when using SS# for the first time.
Thereafter, only one ID# is required. **Mail to:** Christian Growth Study Plan, 127 Ninth Ave., North, Nashville, TN 37234-0117. Fax: (615)251-5067